breaking
THE
TAPE

*Going the Distance
with Purpose Driven
Leadership*

CLIFF KARTHAUSER

foreword by Larry Zimpleman

BREAKING THE TAPE

Cross Training Publishing
www.crosstrainingpublishing.com
(308) 293-3891

The cover photo was taken in May of 1978 as Cliff Karthauser was breaking the tape, winning the first Lincoln Marathon.

ABOUT THE AUTHOR

Cliff Karthauser, CLU, CHFC, CLF, spent 35 years of his professional career in Executive Leadership with The Principal Financial Group. He ended his career with 25 MART "Management Achievement Round Table" qualifications and was inducted into Principal's Leadership Hall of Fame in 2002. Cliff now serves as a Leadership Consultant and Executive Coach.

DEDICATION

I dedicate this book, "Breaking the Tape" to my dad Clete. You left an indelible mark on the lives of many and modeled what purpose driven leadership is all about. Your counsel and wisdom continue to be a guiding light in my life.

ACKNOWLEDGMENTS

To my Mother, Lila, thanks Mom for your constant love and support, and for giving me a swift kick in the rear in the early years. I know I probably deserved it.

To my wife, Patty, thanks for traveling life's journey with me with passion and purpose. Your love and compassion continue to be a blessing in my life and the lives of many.

To my children, Kristin, Laura, and Garrett, you have brought incredible happiness and joy to my life. Continue to be on purpose and make a difference in the lives of those you serve.

To my sister, Rhonda, whose strong quiet courage and sacrificial giving serves not only our family, but so many others.

To my brother, Gar, thanks for walking side by side with me and believing it's the people we lead that matter most. It was a great ride.

And to my nephew, Kyle, this book would not have come to life without your guidance and support. Thanks for sharing this journey with me.

FOREWORD

As I was preparing to write this foreword, I thought it would be helpful to know how many books on leadership are available today. At Amazon alone, there were 187,675 books on leadership! So, does the world need one more book on leadership—absolutely yes, when a proven and passionate leader like Cliff Karthauser decides to share some of his life philosophies through this book.

Many books on leadership are written by academics that have studied (and taught) leadership or by consultants based on their experiences over their career. Many fewer books on leadership are written by people that have actually "done it"—and few have been as successful in their leadership efforts as Cliff Karthauser. I've known Cliff for at least 30 years—first, just as an incredibly gifted runner participating on Corporate Cup track teams where Cliff would not only be the best runner on our team but really was the "heartbeat" of our team—encouraging everyone to perform at their best and modeling that through his own performances. But, shortly thereafter, I began to see Cliff in his "day job" of leading a large group of financial advisers. Note that I said "leading" not "managing" which is how it's often done. I saw Cliff care about EVERY adviser and their career. I saw a leader that was there every day to support his team in any way that he could. And the people that worked with Cliff returned that support through a loyalty to him and our company that was unparalleled. In short, I've never seen a sales leader as gifted as Cliff.

But Cliff is so much more than a gifted sales leader. He (and his wife Patty) live their life with passion and purpose–and this book will share much of that story. Some people "float" through life–but as you will see in this book, Cliff's goal is to inspire others and to help them become the best that they possibly can be.

Leadership is changing today. We have three generations in the workplace–Baby Boomers, Gen X and Gen Y or millennials. Each generation has those leadership traits that they value and look for in their chosen place of employment. Millennials are 80-100% of the new workers being hired into companies today. And they're looking for very specific things in their employment–flexible workspaces, ability to work in collaborative and supportive environments and most importantly, to work for a company that is "making a difference" in what it does. That means environmental sustainability, volunteer opportunities and giving back to the communities where it operates. In short, they want to know "why" their work is important; not just "what" it is they are doing. That's why this book is important and timely.

In short, Millennials are looking for passion-driven leadership. And those companies that will be the winners in the long term are those companies that understand what passion driven leadership means and are helping all of their leaders to understand and embrace the elements of passion driven leadership.

I was thrilled when Cliff told me he was writing a book on leadership. Given my time as a CEO of a company with 15,000 employees, I've seen many leaders–but none that are as passionate and committed to their people as Cliff. I encourage everyone reading this book to think deeply about the role they have today and how "passion driven leadership" can help them move their team or their company to a much higher level of performance—and in doing that, create a workplace where everyone is thrilled to come to work each day because they absolutely know they are making a difference.

Thanks, Cliff, for sharing your story and experiences. You will continue to be an example of passion driven leadership and a role model for all of us that know you and have been influenced by you.

Larry Zimpleman
Former Chairman, CEO and President
Principal Financial Group

INTRODUCTION

Only a year ago, I retired from a 35-year career as a financial services executive for Principal Financial Group. I started as a financial advisor at the age of 26, primarily helping individuals and small businesses set and achieve the financial goals that were important to them. I ended my career as the Regional Managing Director of the Mountain Plains Region. The organization I was responsible for spanned five states and 26 office locations. The Principal Financial Group empowered me with the responsibility to lead with passion, purpose, and clarity of vision. On a day-to-day basis, this is accomplished in meetings, on the phone, at conferences and summer retreats; often, it takes the form of e-mails and strategic planning sessions, and small talk about the weekend, or office gatherings with paper plates and a birthday cake. It was a journey not unlike a marathon, requiring long-term vision and focus, but accomplished one step at a time.

Lately I find myself reflecting on the life journey that brought me to this moment. I've tried to learn from all the experiences and opportunities God has provided. I find myself becoming introspective, contemplating the purpose of my life, the lessons I drew upon and tried to teach as a leader, and the nature of my legacy. As my grandkids would say, "Poppy, you're getting old!" While that's probably part of it, I think we all want life to matter. We all want to leave behind some kind of legacy.

At times we have the good fortune to be able to reflect on the sum value of our life in a moment of stillness, retrospectively. But often we are faced with it in a moment of unexpected disruption. In the latter case the evaluation we make is not a luxury but a life changing circumstance: It will literally determine the shape of our lives in the next week, our next day, our next moment.

Breaking the Tape is not so much about the legacy per se, but how to think about the choices we make that shape it on a day-to-day basis. Part of it is my story–the story of a young man who found his passion in long-distance running and was tested by the death of his father. It's also the story of Jon Schuetz, another young man who, in the prime of his life, suffered a near fatal motorcycle accident that fractured his fourth and fifth cervical vertebrae and Quality Living, Inc., the rehabilitation center that helped him recover. It's about the four pillars of Passion, Purpose, Vision, and Mission, which I think can help carry us through life, wherever it may take us.

I think it's important for all of us to reflect on our own journey with passion, purpose, and clarity of vision. And when we break the tape, to remember the race isn't over. But to think about the kind of legacy we truly want to leave.

How do you put into words what transpires in the span of 35 years? It's an interesting book filled with many highs and a few lows.

CONTENTS

Section 1
Beginnings

1
My Inner Circle

I was born and raised in Lincoln Nebraska, in a very traditional, loving household. Mom stayed home, made breakfast, and got me and my younger sister and brother off to school. Then she did laundry, maybe some shopping, and kept tabs on what was happening in the neighborhood. At night, after preparing dinner, she called us to come inside, wash up, and eat. Then she did the dishes and after that she made sure we were clean from our toes to behind our ears and put us to bed. Dad ate breakfast in the morning, worked and came home, ate dinner, then smoked a cigarillo. This was growing up in the late 50s, into the 60s and 70s. I graduated from High School in 1971, graduated from college in 1975.

Like I said, it was a traditional, loving household. But let's not sell it short by calling it normal—all of us who are parents know that just hitting the "normal" mark is tough. My mother and father both excelled at it.

My mother Lila grew up on a farm. Every morning she was out milking cows, whether it was 90 degrees in August or -15 in January. Every day she was churning out butter, or collecting eggs, or driving the truck into town with her Dad. Between morning and evening chores, she went to school. At night she had to do more than a young woman's share of housework as her mother was often bedridden. Lila worked hard as a nail most of her life because hard work got you to the bare minimum of getting by.

I've never seen my mother shrink from doing something that needed to be done. Not once have I heard her say, "That's not my job!" To this day, like many of her generation who came out of the Great Depression, she's always keeping her eye out for a deal on toilet paper and bananas. She was part of a generation that was always thankful for what it had because it knew what it meant to go without.

I see a lot of my Grandpa in my mother. Mom was close with both parents, but she had a special relationship with Grandpa as most girls have with their fathers. Grandpa took great care of Mom during her formative years, and he instilled in both Mom and her brother the importance of strong family and faith based values. And in the later stages of his life, when his health began to decline, Mom returned the favor and took care of him. I spent a lot of time on the farm as a young boy. I saw these values modeled by Grandpa throughout his entire life. The lessons I learned were many, whether it was going to Grandpa's favorite fishing hole or riding for hours with him on the fender of his John Deere tractor or going to the local grocery store and having Grandpa hand me a quarter to pick out my favorite candy. Over the years Grandpa had many dogs. And each time a new one showed up they became my favorite. But there is no arguing about the fact that Smokey was my real favorite. Smokey was my dog and it was fun to hear Grandpa say to people, I think Smokey likes my grandson more than me and I'm the one that feeds him every day. It's funny as we get older the things we remember most vividly.   At the time, I wasn't thinking about the life lessons I was learning on the farm. But now I know that my Grandpa was one of the most passionate purpose-driven individuals I had the privilege to learn from and call Grandpa.

Cletus, my Dad, had to work hard too. His father was an alcoholic and not good for much. Actually, good for nothing. When Cletus was 9 or 10, his father walked out the door never to be heard from again. Disappeared–no explanation, no note; literally as though he walked off the face of the earth. Left behind my dad, another son, two daughters, and his wife. After that, they struggled to get by, and their household came to be known as "the poor house" in McCook, Nebraska.

My dad learned a lot from his mother, growing up in a single-mother home. They lived in a small two bedroom house. My grandmother would make bread and then my father would go door-to-door selling the loaves so they could pay the rent. Grandma always had her rosary beads at the ready. My grandmother was fervently Catholic and the household was extremely strict. Growing up for Cletus was something of a trial.

When he graduated from high school he joined the Marine Corps. The Korean War was on. During his four years in the service he would send checks home to his mother to help make ends meet. After the war, he came back to Lincoln and began his career with the Nebraska State Patrol.

When my mother and father met, they married within months. The wedding was in Lincoln, and it was not Catholic, and the only relative that my father invited was his sister. I never got the chance to ask him about it, but looking back I wonder why he did that. My father was not happy in that household. Somehow he knew that he didn't fit within his family culture and that he couldn't change it. He knew that there was far more to life than the situation he was born into had to offer. There were better opportunities, better ways of raising a family; more happiness and more freedom. He knew this instinctively and it shows, I think, remarkable vision and courage. Finding my mother and getting out of McCook, those were accomplishments back then. But they couldn't have known how successful they would eventually be together.

Following on the heels of his military service he decided to try a job as a State Trooper with the Nebraska State Patrol. He started from the bottom of the organization in a new town, with virtually no connections, nothing more to his name than a high school education and military service, and over the next 23 years, he advanced through the ranks clear up to Superintendent Colonel of the Nebraska State Patrol. This is a position directly appointed by the governor.

All this by the age of 45. Today, any Colonel would have a college education, a degree in business or criminal justice. But leadership is not defined by a title–it's not a position, it's an activity. It's how you carry yourself. It's the culture you cultivate within your organization. Every day, people from all walks of life go out and lead. Sometimes it's at work–in small teams at a cleaning company, as a principal overseeing a student body and staff, or as a police officer on the beat. Sometimes leadership plays out in our personal lives. Every day, parents get up early and make breakfast for their family, strangers go out of their way to help each other, big sisters look out for their little brothers. These are all examples of leadership–teaching by example, inculcating good habits and values and weeding out the bad. Leadership isn't restricted to a conference room or heads of state on the world stage. Leadership is about impact, influence, and inspiration.

Summing Up

My parents' greatest accomplishments? From my perspective, the top three are creating a good name, making sure that their three kids were able to go to college–and we were the first, both on my mother's and father's side–and leave it debt-free, and all the short-term sacrifices that they made throughout their life to lay the foundation for their kids to have happy and successful lives.

My parents were my pillars, my support. And they had their own pillars, their own wellsprings of experience, and their own culture going back generations. On my mom's side, the culture she came from demanded hard work and self-reliance, but also taught her to have fun, to be thankful for what she had. On my dad's side, many of the negative aspects of his environment spurred him to change his life in a fundamental way. From a pretty deep low in his childhood he ascended to great heights.

I have tried to live up to their standard as a father to my three children, and now as a grandfather to four. When you're growing up, you don't really sense the lessons as they come. Looking back now, all the defining moments of my life are clear. It's a little bit like the skin of a tree. When a tree is young, the bark is smooth and unblemished. But with every season comes a new challenge—wind, rain, hail, frost, heat. One day you come back to the tree and the bark is gnarled and notched from the roots to the highest branches. Life lessons are like that: the texture of your experiences doesn't come into focus until a lifetime has passed.

Now I'm trying to pay attention to the lessons that have been ingrained in me. The value of a good name, the importance of your spiritual journey, and staying on the straight and narrow—the work that requires. Helping others. Always doing your best. Respecting yourself. I wonder if, at some point in their own lives they acknowledged their own pillars, their own vision, passion, mission, and purpose. We all have a purpose and a passion that transcends the everyday. For my parents, that was to do better than their parents before them, as much for themselves as for their children. The passion and purpose of my parents has made all the difference in my life. Without the dedication and love of my parents, I wouldn't be where I am today.

2
GOING THE DISTANCE

Athletics has been the second biggest influence on my life, after my parents. Athletics was my first true passion. Aside from the Big Moments of life—getting married, having children, losing loved ones—my moments in sports are those that I remember most clearly. "Remember" might not even be a strong enough word. A few of the marathons I've run are still so crystal-clear in my mind that I can recall all the cramps and stitches in my side, where they happened, how much time they took off my pace, and how long it took me to recover.

So where does passion like this come from? Was I born with a better set of legs and lungs than most people, and running just "fit" me? Maybe. But I think it had more to do with my coaches, the support my family gave me, and the culture of competition that was instilled within me over the years. I had reasonable running talent that showed itself in during- and after-school activities. But not until a high school cross country coach named Max Hester visited my junior high did I have any sense that sport went beyond recreation. I don't recall the details of his talk so much as the impact it had on me. He called on us to perform and excel in a way that I had never heard in math or English class. I thought, "You know what? I've had a little success running in gym class in junior high. Why not give cross country a try?"

Looking back, it was inevitable that I'd give track and cross country a shot. My best friend growing up was Ronny Greeno, whose Dad was Nebraska Wesleyan University's Athletics Director, as well as their track and cross-country coach. Ronny and his family lived right across the street from Dawes Elementary and Junior High. We were classmates all the way from kindergarten to college. We did all the usual stuff together growing up, including track, basketball, and cross-country, but the really special moments always involved Ron's Dad, Woody. Sometimes on the weekends Woody took us to Wesleyan, unlocked the gym, and let us shoot hoops. Eventually we got so comfortable being on campus that, after school, we'd walk the mile from Dawes School to the university to watch the college athletes practice and run drills. That was a pretty big deal to us little farts! But they were nothing compared to the times when, having ordered new equipment for the upcoming season, Woody would have me in to pick out a pair of brand new running shoes.

Fast-forward to my sophomore year of high school, and I've gone from a scrawny kid who liked to do laps on the playground to a scrawny kid who somehow managed to make the varsity cross country squad. We had a very good team that year, led by a couple of seniors, a few juniors, and two or three very good sophomore runners. As I remember, we ended up with sixth place at state that year. And in my junior year we got even better. We moved from being sixth in the state my sophomore year to being third my junior year. So we went into our senior campaign poised to make a run at the state title. That was our goal.

It may seem like we're in the weeds to some extent with all these details, but in my own life the transition from not running competitively to running competitively was as stark as the night turning into the day. We all have phases in our life that, once complete, become the natural and fitting foundation for the next. Running was my second phase, and it lay firmly on the first, which was composed purely of the love, encouragement, and support from my family.

If you can cast yourself back to those days, you will remember that local sports news was news. Newspaper clippings from meets and basketball games are still carried around in our family scrapbooks. You can read a breakdown of who scored which points, where they shot from, how many shots they made versus how many they missed; you can read highlights of crucial moments in the game; players, coaches, fans, and staff are interviewed. Back then, a good weekend in Nebraska didn't consist of going to a new movie or the mall. Everyone was at their respective high school (or their rival's) watching a game, followed by a grill out or ice cream if you were lucky. Most families have their golden years growing up, and these were ours.

Going back to the state title—that was my goal. That was my team's goal. It was my coach's goal for the group. It was our school's goal. It was my family's goal for me. Can you think of a more powerful motivator than to be surrounded by people who want the same thing as you? A whole community focused on the same goal. Good luck to anyone who tries to get in the way of that. I don't want to blow this out of proportion too much—whether we won or

lost here, there was nothing really at stake. But as a life lesson, as a lesson in motivation and leadership, I can't fail to
mention that aligning interests toward a common goal is
the first and last lesson of leadership.

We trained our guts out in preparation for that senior
campaign. We prepared hard all summer. We began the
year and had great success at our first meet. We were undefeated. As a matter of fact, beyond undefeated: we had several meets where we ran the table and had perfect scores.
Now, back then, in cross-country, at some of the small
meets you ran seven athletes and scored your top five runners. At state, you ran your top five runners and you scored
four. Well, many of the meets, the smaller meets, we would
finish 1-2-3-4-5 and we would have a perfect score. This
was the fall of 1970. There was not one runner from another team that would place between our team runners. To
this day, there's not been another cross-country team in
the history of Nebraska high school athletics that has had
the kind of run we had in our senior campaign.

Woody

Upon graduating high school, I began to see how running was opening up my world. Literally my entire life up
to that point had taken place within a square mile portion
of northeast Lincoln. Thanks to the success of my high
school athletics, though, I was getting letters from schools
all over the country. That felt great! But I knew that I had
unfinished business to see to and untapped potential to
mine right where I was—with Ron and Woody Greeno.

From the 9th grade on, I had always known in my heart-of-hearts that I was going to go to Nebraska Wesleyan University.

Why? Well, at the time, it didn't have anything to do with their academic reputation. I couldn't have written three sentences about that. To me, the entire institution boiled down to one man: Woody Greeno. Over the years, he had become a kind of father figure to me. He was the mentor who ushered me from boyhood to manhood through the crucible of cross-country running.

To the cross country and track athletes who attended Wesleyan, Woody Greeno was bigger than life. Not by stature, as he stood only 5-foot-8, but by reputation and the fact of his presence. He wore his passion for us and for the sport on his sleeve, and he demanded a lot–loyalty to him, to each other; dedication physically and mentally–but he always kept you guessing. Sometimes it was with a colorful but baffling crudity about *just* how cold it was outside, or a sudden dressing-down in front of the team. But this was balanced out by unbridled joy and affection after all of his team broke the tape at our senior conference championship. And at the end of the season, he disappeared to his farm in South Dakota for the summer, only returning a week before the start of the new school year.

Woody wasn't the most technically skilled coach, but he was a master motivator. He always got the best out of his athletes because they didn't want to disappoint him. I had a distinct advantage when I began my college career because I grew up as part of the Greeno family.

Over the years, I developed a strong bond with Woody.

I walked into our first practice as a freshman knowing his bark was bigger than his bite. He was a simple man, a throwback, an old school coach. A few of his demands were gospel, in the Old Testament sense—basic, inflexible, and strict. He demanded respect. He expected us always to show up for practice on time. He demanded that we be prepared mentally and physically. He could also exude warmth that taught you to have love in your heart for your teammates and respect for your competitors. But like I said, he was old school, and the lesson first and foremost for running and for life was to fear no one.

I can still see him, standing in the infield, his trademark pipe in his shirt pocket or in his mouth. I can still hear him shouting at us between puffs. And I will always be able to remember the smell of the pipe smoke as we closed in on Woody for a talk after finishing drills, greeting me with: "Clifford. Your eyes look like two piss holes in a snow bank." That was Woody. I wanted to run for him. Everyone who trained under Woody wanted to run so badly for him, they'd plow through a brick wall if he asked. He saw a lot in me, and I knew I wanted to spend my four years of college athletics with him.

The hard training I did for my first year at Wesleyan wasn't just because I wanted to prove myself to someone. This wasn't just about principles and making a good impression. Above all, it was *work*. Every ounce of sweat you put into preparation translated directly into the time it took to break the tape at the end of the race. Back then, if you did cross country in high school, you were running two-mile distances. In college, it was five. So Ron and I had been running two-mile distances for three years and now we're more than doubling that on a regular basis. But that played to my advantage. I was not born with a lot of natural leg speed; that was something I had to work really hard on. But I could go the distance. So my raw talent was an asset in the five mile world, but right from the start I knew that if I was going to reach my full potential, I was going to have to be disciplined about my training, and make a commitment to out-train everyone else. All this drove me to a great freshman season.

Like I said, I was flying pretty high. This renewed determination and a growing sense of my abilities led me to think that all the wind in my sails wasn't from behind. And the headwinds came from an ironic source: my best friend Ron Greeno. Not once, in all three years in high school, did I ever beat Ron. Never. And this carried over into my freshman year of college. Throughout, my parents would talk to me about having a mental block. They would say, "You have as much talent as Ron, you have as much ability as Ron. There's no reason that you should always finish second to him." And to make matters worse, the thing that separated my second-place finish from Ron's first-place was a few seconds. In the last three- or four-hundred yards, he would speed up a bit and break the tape right in front of me.

This continued even into the five-mile races in college. We both made the varsity team as freshmen, and scored in every meet, but I would always finish 3, 4, 5 seconds behind Ron. Now, this was not for good reason. Ron was a tremendous runner. Tremendous leg speed. To this day, his high school mile time still ranks as one of the fastest ever recorded in Nebraska.

Whenever my parents would mention the mental block, I would get really angry and argue with them. But looking back on it now, I know that they were right. As to what the nature of that block was, why it was there–who can know? But what I do know is how I got over it. Five years into Ron and my running careers, in the summer between my sophomore and junior years, there was an incredible improvement in my running. Woody noticed it. And being the great coach and mentor that he was, he knew when and how to acknowledge it for best effect. How? It was very simple, and I remember it like it was yesterday. Woody pulled me aside and said, "Clifford. It's okay. It's your time. It's your time. You need to take the torch and you need to break the tape." I'm not sure that he ever knew the emotional impact that had on me at the time, or just how he knew when to say it, but it was exactly what I needed. That marked the last time that Ron ever finished in front of me.

I went on to a stellar junior year, winning many of the cross-country meets in which I had the opportunity to compete. I finished fifth at the NCAA National cross-country championships that year and made All-American status. In the track season, I also had a very good campaign which culminated in a third place finish in the three-mile run at the national college track and field championships, qualifying again as All-American. I trained hard going into my senior campaign and was poised to finish my collegiate eligibility with a goal of breaking the tape in every race I entered.

Pride is a funny thing. We all want to accomplish things, to stand out for great work or accomplishments, to be recognized for what makes us unique. Many of us wake up and go to sleep every single day craving a sense of achievement. But when that recognition comes, you may find a little goes a long way—and too much may mess with your head. This was a lesson I learned during my senior campaign. The national cross-country championships were on the Chicago Country Club golf course in Wheaton, Illinois. So the team went up to Chicago for the event and, wouldn't you know it—one of the newspapers there was running a story about it. I picked it up and there I was, chosen as the odds-on favorite to win the national championship. At the same event my junior year, I had finished fifth. So I got nervous. I had the whole day to think about it. I slept very poorly that night, fighting off waves of amazement—"Holy cow, they really think I'm good enough to win this thing,"—and dread—"Holy cow, everybody's expecting me to win this thing." At some point I fell asleep. In the very next instant (or so it seemed), I was awake and heading out the door for the race. I finished seventh. Not a good race at all. What's worse, I didn't measure up to what was expected of me.

Winning gives you confidence, of course, but I drew confidence from my training as well. The time I put into training gave me the confidence that I could compete with anyone. Prior to the National meet, I had a workout I knew put me in a position to become National Champion. And this day began as all others, with a seven-mile morning run. During our afternoon practice, we ran six one-mile repeats with a five-minute rest period between each one. I ran all six repeat miles under 4:40 per mile. The key to the practice was that each mile would be faster than the previous. My fifth mile repeat was 4:27, and my sixth and last was 4:25. Isn't it incredible to this day that I still remember that workout? It still stands out in my mind. This workout not only prepared me physically, but mentally as well. I knew I was ready for Nationals.

But things don't always work out as we plan. That's how life goes, isn't it? You start out as a small fish in a big pond. If you keep your head down and stay focused, eventually you get your moment in the sun. You take a big leap, you're flying through the air, you look down and think, "That isn't more than a puddle!" You hardly have time to appreciate the view before you abruptly splash down into another pond where, once again, you're just a small fish. The key thing here is you can learn from your successes as well as your setbacks. Whatever your current situation, ninety percent of your energy should always go toward maintaining the sphere of self-discipline necessary to stay in the game, at a higher and higher level. Always remember that it's the journey, not the destination. Sooner or later, your circumstances will match up perfectly with your skill level and you'll know that your preparation has provided you with opportunities to succeed. All it takes is one success to get you through a hundred failures. If you're failing, you know you have room to grow. If you're succeeding, you know it's time to push through to even greater heights; to set new goals.

Part of my success boiled down to good fortune. I was

fortunate to have Woody Greeno as my coach. He saw that even though I was a small fish, I could be a bigger one someday. He picked me out of the crowd, kept his eye on me, encouraged and helped when he could, and he challenged me when the going was too easy. I attribute a lot of the success I've had in business and in life to the fact that Woody Greeno believed in me. Ironically, his belief in me also pushed me to go beyond what he wanted for me. If he were here now, I'm sure he would laugh at that last phrase–"go beyond what he wanted." Actually, what might be the most important decision in my entire sports career was an act of clear insubordination to Woody. But what else is a college senior from Nebraska supposed to do when given free tickets to the big game? Stay home?

Marathon Running: A Career of Passion

The story of my running career isn't as straightforward as I've presented it so far. To tell the whole thing, we have to rewind a bit. In reality, there are two parallel stories. The first had to do with learning to run, cultivating my inner discipline, and going to run for Woody Greeno. The other story is all about my decisions, my pacing, my dreams.

I ran my first marathon in the summer of my sophomore year of college. I went up to Brookings, South Dakota to compete in what was called "The Longest Day Marathon." It was held on a long, square blacktop highway. So you would go many miles one-way, turn, and so on, until you had run 26 miles. I was fortunate enough to win that marathon prior to my junior campaign. And then I ran my second marathon in August of 1974. This was prior to my senior cross-country campaign. That was the very first Omaha Marathon, and the first in Nebraska. I won that one too—but this one was special, because the winner received an all-expense paid trip to the Boston Marathon the following April. Well, Boston was about five or six weeks before our team's conference track meet, and you shouldn't be running a marathon right in the middle of the track season. But this was such a big deal to me, winning this all-expense paid trip. I had never been on an airplane! So I won the Omaha Marathon, got on the plane, and ran the marathon in Boston in April of 1975, against my coach's wishes. He was vehemently opposed to me going to Boston and running a marathon just a few weeks before our track and field conference championship. He said I wouldn't recover in time; it'd affect the rest of my track season—on and on. This is what 99% of the world's population would advise you to do in this situation, because no matter what shape you're in, running 26 miles in one go is tough on your body. But I went and did it anyway, fulfilling a dream I had always had.

The dream went something like this: A college senior gets on the first airplane of his life. The plane takes him to Boston, the biggest city he's ever been to in his life. He checks into a hotel all by himself. He wakes up and suits up for his first international sporting event. He's 2-0 for marathons, both in cities that aren't on most people's radar screens. Yet there he is, at the line, stretching with Olympic-level runners. He finds a place at the line. The gun sounds. All the runners take off. Two hours and twenty-one minutes later, he's one of the top 30 finishers.

Sometimes I still have to remind myself that it wasn't a dream. That was one of those moments where dream and reality mixed for me. I had no designs on being a top finisher in that race. Just being there was a prize in and of itself. I've run dozens of marathons now, but back then, I didn't know anything about it: the pain, the psychological fortitude and agony, eating right, proper shoes, regulating water intake. I was running on instinct and adrenaline and naiveté. It was all so surreal—especially my time. Two hours and twenty-one minutes was a whole *ten minutes* better than my best time. That's extraordinary in the running world. I was on cloud nine after that. What could kill *that* buzz?

Going back to Nebraska, as it turned out. Woody told me how proud he was of me, but, exactly as he had predicted, I ran very poorly in the next few meets. I was still on such a runner's high after running in Boston, the losses didn't faze me at first. But the conference championships were approaching. The conference championships of my senior year. That is to say, my last year running at the collegiate level.

Whoops

All of a sudden I had to come to terms with what I had done. And I had to adjust in every way to try to position myself appropriately for my team and to end my season and collegiate career well. I had to push myself to find the limits. What makes this a defining moment for me was not that I overreached, stumbled, and failed to break the tape.

It's that I reached further than I ever had before and found myself keeping pace. I paid for it, sure, but it's not often in life that you can re-define your view of what's possible.

So I had my bright, shining moment at the Boston Marathon. Then I got knocked around at a few track meets where I was used to being top dog. I just kept my head down and powered through. Several days before we were due to board the buses to the NCAA National track meet in Cleveland, I got the life back in my legs. I felt like a new person. I wasn't one hundred percent, but soon I would be.

I had qualified to compete in both the 3-mile and 6 mile at Nationals. In the 3 mile you had to run a qualifying heat in order to make the finals. This was a blessing for me, as it gave me more time to recover. The 3-mile finals were on Saturday and the 6-mile finals were on Friday evening. So I had to pace myself very carefully in the 3-mile prelims, which were on Thursday. My sole goal in the 3-mile pre-liminaries was to run just fast enough to make the finals on Saturday. There were two heats and the top eight runners in each heat qualified for the finals. I finished 3rd or 4th in my heat, punching my ticket for the finals. So far, so good. On Friday I laced up my running shoes for the 6-mile finals. I remember the race well. During the early stages of the race I positioned myself in the first group of runners, never further back than 4th or 5th. With about 800 meters to go, I took the lead followed by a runner from Brandeis University. We began to separate ourselves from the pack so I knew with two laps to go it was going to come down to me being National Champion or finishing 2nd. I wasn't blessed with particularly great closing leg speed, so I knew

I had to have a sustained drive to the finish. I picked up the pace and started my kick. If I was going to lose, I was determined not to get out-kicked the last 100 meters. I was able to open up a gap and I broke the tape a full 6 seconds ahead of the second place runner.

Woody just about lost his voice hollering during that race. He came rushing over from the sidelines after the finish to tell me that I was National Champion in the six-mile run—only the second Nebraska Wesleyan athlete to win a national championship.

Next Steps

As I left the university, I worked that summer, and married my wife Patty on August 2nd of 1975. We celebrated our 40th anniversary last August. We got married in Omaha, where she grew up. I had accepted a position with the FBI in Washington, D.C. Having grown up in a law enforcement family this felt natural to me. Patty was accepted into American University to pursue a Ph.D. program in physiological psychology. So we packed up what we had at the time and drove across the country, the trunk and backseat full of what we had to take with us, to begin our married life in Washington, D.C. We lived there for three years. I hooked up with a high powered running club, the Washington Running Club, and we competed all over the East Coast in road races and running events.

Patty and I didn't know anybody in D.C. I missed my family tremendously, and Patty did as well. We had the opportunity after 3 years to move back to Lincoln. So after starting my career with the federal government we moved back, and I transitioned into the Nebraska State Attorney General's office as an antitrust investigator. But really, during the time I spent in D.C. and the two years that I spent in the attorney general's office, my primary focus was still on my running career. I had accomplished a lot in college, and I was eager to pursue a post-collegiate running career.

Though we had worried about what we would be leaving behind on the East Coast—city life and all of the culture and activity that surrounds it, job opportunities, new friends—when we arrived back in Nebraska, we knew we had made the right decision for us. In D.C., Patty had moved into computer analysis as a profession, so it was easy for her to find a professional position in the Midwest. We both had many roots there, and her twin sister was nearby in Omaha. It felt natural to fall back into the routine of seeing my folks, going to my brother's athletic events, and spending time with my sister.

Just as I was getting into my own personal marathon groove, it turned out that the country was, too. Lincoln, Nebraska held its first marathon soon after we moved back, on the first Sunday in May of 1978. In that first event there were only 350 athletes. Today, it's grown to be something like 13,500 runners. That's pretty amazing in a community the size of Lincoln.

By now, I knew why I was good at marathon running. I knew what I liked about it. I had continued to run at a pretty high level and, actually, the marathon was probably my best event. The marathon distance fit me, as I was able to carry a good pace for an extended distance. In this particular marathon, I ran 2:19:43. Second place clocked in at 2:34:25. To this day, my winning margin of nearly 15 minutes still ranks as the greatest gap between the first and second finisher in a marathon.

Being 15 minutes ahead of the next competitor makes for a lonely race. Thankfully, my brother and brother-in-law rode along with me on ten speed bikes. My dad and wife Patty were there at certain points to cheer me on. And one of the things about my parents: they never, ever missed an athletic event, or a choral event, or a play—for me; or my brother Gary, he was a very accomplished basketball player and runner in his early years; or for my sister who was involved in sports and a lot of school activities. What I remember extremely well to this day is that my parents were always there to support the interests and activities of all their children. Rarely did they miss anything; they were always there to encourage us and to lend their support.

During the Lincoln Marathon, it's such a long distance—my Mom told me ahead of time, "I can't go, I can't see you suffer like that." But my Dad was there with bells on. My dad was at every event he could possibly go to. I really cherish the memory of that marathon for a few reasons. I had recently returned home with my wife from the East Coast; my brother rode beside me the whole way, just me and him; and my dad and wife were there, cheering from the checkpoints.

The embrace Dad gave me at the end of that marathon was no different than any other he'd ever given me, but it's one I'll never forget. That was in May of 1978. We lost him the following April. April 8, 1979. It happened to be Palm Sunday. I got a call at five in the morning from my brother, extremely upset. He told me that Dad had had a heart attack.

"How bad is it?"

"It's pretty bad, they're taking him to the hospital now."

I threw my jeans and a t-shirt on and woke up Patty. I remember the ride over, the heaviness and the thickness of the emotion. Patty was eight months pregnant with our first child. The news that I both expected and feared was waiting for us at the hospital.

I lost my Dad. I lost my mentor in life. Our rock, anchor, comforter, voice of reason; the life of the party, the jokester, the head of the State Patrol. Dad had a special touch. A rare kind of light shined from within him. To everyone around him, Dad was bigger than life. He was a pillar of our community, too. So well respected within the law enforcement ranks, the church, the neighborhood... I wasn't sure how we were going to survive. I wasn't sure how my mother would survive. How would she fill that gaping hole in her life and her heart? And how would she make ends meet? My mom had never had a real job; my brother was in school; my sister had just graduated from college. I had my first child on the way. My mom was going to have her first grandchild right after losing her partner. My child was never going to know her grandfather. It's amazing how still the world gets when something like that happens, when you feel like you're drowning on your feet. Even the clear blue sky felt raw after we emerged from the hospital, after we lost Cletus Karthauser at 51 years old. Thank God we still had each other.

The funeral was the following Wednesday. Over a thousand people attended. Military and law enforcement personnel from all over the Midwest came to pay their respects. The church was overflowing, so chairs were set up outside. Then they ran out of chairs and people just stood. I remember the rifle salute, the rows of uniformed officers, the presentation and folding of the flag. It'll always feel like it was only yesterday that it all happened, and yet a lifetime has passed.

What was really difficult were the days following that. The days after. Our biggest concern was for our mother, you know, was she going to be okay? Lila lost her best friend, her partner in life. It was the biggest challenge she had ever had to face. One of the emotional saving graces for Mom was the fact that her first granddaughter was born about a month after Dad passed away. This little bundle of joy was my first daughter, Kristin. Just a wonderful baby, a beautiful child, and my mother poured an ocean of emotion and time into her. The timing of Kristin's birth was a miracle for our family.

Life goes on—somehow. Death is profound like that: inside, everything has changed. Outside, the world hasn't even skipped a beat. You wake up in the morning and you don't know what to do with your life, even if it's already pretty structured. "Eat breakfast? Go to work? Wash the car? What for?" For me, a big one was, "Why run?"

When my Dad passed, I had been preparing for the 1979 Boston Marathon. This one was special because a fast enough time would qualify me for the 1980 US Olympic Trials. That was tremendously important to me. Some people run for local office and dream of being President. Others run marathons and dream of being in the Olympics. Well, the Boston Marathon was a week after Dad died. Just days after his funeral.

I had trained for that event with a steely-eyed focus for an entire year. A whole year of dreams about representing my country in the world's biggest sporting competition now had all the heft and luster of cast-off cardboard. Forty-eight hours after burying Dad, I was supposed to be on a plane to Boston. And because Patty was eight-months pregnant, I was going alone. You try to go through the motions, so I pulled out a suitcase to pack. But acting as if nothing had happened was too painful. And yet not going–to not do something I had been preparing for, was painful. I put the suitcase away.

Soon after the funeral, Mom called me into her living room. She knew what I was going through. She said, "You know what Dad would want you to do. He was so proud of you. He was so proud of all your accomplishments. He's going to be looking down on you and you know the decision that he wants you to make." Then my brother told me that he had bought a plane ticket to Boston. He was going to go with me. Suddenly, grief turned to resolution. Instead of sapping all color and meaning from the world, my Dad's death made everything that much more urgent. How could I *not* run?

Getting to Boston–that was a feat. Running the marathon–that was difficult. It always is. But this time I had my Dad with me in every stride that I took. And though there were tens of thousands of people there, enormous crowds, banners, flags, noise from the crowd, police sirens, bullhorns, news crews, ambulances… I might as well have been alone, running through a tunnel where the sound of every footfall soaked up in that strange blend of exhilaration and agony, of tension and release. Twenty-six miles is a long way to drive. It's a really long way to run. There's a zen quality to controlling your thoughts, your stride, your breathing. Imagining a stopwatch clocking each mile marker before you get there. Break the tape in your mind. Do it again. Again. Again. Do the mile that you just ran. Again. Adjust the time of your next three markers because you've got a stitch in your side. Skip water this mile. You have to be in the cockpit, your hand on each and every control there is—but you also have to be relaxed and patient. You have to push yourself and yet let yourself disappear. The finish line crawls toward you. *Dad is gone. Keep running.* Your whole body is reduced to the rhythmic ache of your footfalls. The volume kicks back in; there are people everywhere, all around you. *2:17:18. Personal record. Qualified for the Olympic Trials by four minutes. Water.* A huge wall of people behind striped police barriers. *Breathe.* The world starts to come back to you. *The funeral.* As I look for a place to stop, I see my brother, somehow here, having made it over all the barriers, through the police; and before I collapse he's hugging me, clapping my back and hollering, so happy and excited for me. We embraced and we cried, and the pureness of that love, our love and the love for our father—I will take that feeling to my grave, that moment where my heart was beating next to my brother's. We both knew that we could make it, that life could go on, that things would be different without Dad but that it was all okay as long as we still had each other.

The next year I was able to go to Buffalo for the Olympic trials. And by then, my daughter Kristin was a year old. So my mother watched Kristin. She filled a void for my Mom. It's hard for me to imagine what my Mom would have done without a granddaughter then. To this day, she hasn't remarried. There was just no way she was going to find another guy like Dad.

So Kristin stayed behind with mom while Patty, my brother and I headed to Buffalo, New York for the '80 Olympic trials. I had a very good race. There were 250 athletes that met the qualifying standard out of a couple thousand that tried—so it's not a big field, it's not like the Boston or New York Marathon. You have only 250 of the best marathoners in the United States, and I set a personal record of 2:16:15 and finished 24th. The unfortunate thing is, about 4 or 5 miles before the finish, I experienced a severe side cramp that took me about 2 miles to get rid of. It probably cost me about 6 or 7 spots and maybe a minute or two, because it dramatically affected my diaphragm and my ability to breathe. In any case, I was still very happy with my finish; I knew that Dad was looking down on me and my accomplishment and was very proud.

***

There's a poem that means a lot to me:

"because I call it challenge rather than crisis;
because I look at hardship as opportunity instead of obstacle;
because at the end of a matter, I ask,

'what will I learn from this to make me better?';
because I take a deep breath and do the difficult thing first;
because my courage does not depend on the weather, the
economic forecast or the winds of whim;
because I know the most significant elements of my day are
laughter, learning and applying my finest efforts to each endeavor;
because of these things
each morning is a pleasure
and every day passed is a success."
–Mary Anne Radmacher

When I think about my Dad, that poem helps a lot. It helps me to understand that from the hopelessness of crisis a profound courage can emerge—the courage that comes from having made it through. It helps me to see that in the most unbearable pain and anguish there is a purity and a stillness that, faced head-on, can carry you into the winner's circle. As easily as a coin flips from head to tail, the taste of ash in your mouth turns to sweetness beyond imagination. The death of my father was, in retrospect, perfectly balanced by my relationships with my mother, my sister, and my brother, which carried me to new heights of achievement. The death of my father was traumatic, but also made the birth of my first child, my mother's first grandchild, all the more meaningful. The death of my father gave way to a moment of grace that surpassed all prior understanding, and now marks the arc of my whole life's progress as a gentle curve toward a future of love, peace, and hope.

I've continued to run and compete. I've been an ambassador of the sport my entire life and I still run to this day.

I've coached a lot of people who were maybe never athletes in college, who never ran until later in life—but they had a goal of finishing a half-marathon, of becoming more healthy. I've helped a lot of people with those aspirations put a plan together, put a workout regimen together, and really coach and counsel them on what they needed to do to prepare themselves to *participate*—not to win, but participate, to finish, to accomplish something that they set out to do. Because I love the sport and it's been a huge part of my life and to this day it still is.

Section 2
Purpose Redefined

3
A VIEW OF WHAT IS POSSIBLE

That's My Story. We all have our own stories; stories that we tell to ourselves or to each other. I chose to talk about my upbringing, my career in sports, and the death of my father because they are my defining moments. They are the pillars upon which I've built my life. In times of uncertainty, they are constellations in the sky I orient myself by.

We all encounter tests and trials which, when faced, reveal to us our own individual life lessons. For example, success in marathon running required me to develop an ability to focus over long periods of time, to ignore pain, and to visualize near- and short-term goals. What does that have to do with leadership? Just because I was a successful marathon runner, I'm a great manager? No, not necessarily. It has to do with character. First you have to build it, or rather the challenges of life will help you define it. As your own character develops, it begins to guide the choices and decisions you make. And you must also learn to gauge the strengths and character of those around you and guide them to use their strengths to the advantage of your organization. Finding your own passion and purpose, unifying others around a common vision, using the best parts of your character as your North Star—this is the heart of leadership. Translating the lessons and experiences that work well for us on an individual basis into the customs and mores that guide and inspire an organization—that's culture.

Some say it takes a lifetime to truly understand these matters, and they're probably right. But every so often you find yourself in an extraordinary situation that really changes how you see the world. On November 5, 2015 – and many years after I thought I'd learned everything I ever needed to know about myself, management, and leadership–a chance meeting turned into yet another defining moment. I saw how character combined with excellent organizational culture can literally accomplish miracles.

***

November 5th of 2015 started like most days. An early morning workout followed by emails, phone calls, and some motivational reading to put me in a positive frame of mind for the day. That afternoon I was hosting a leadership retreat for a group of emerging leaders in Omaha. Included as part of the retreat was a visit to Quality Living, Inc. (QLI), a brain and spinal cord injury rehabilitation center in Omaha. We heard from their President and CEO, Patricia Kearns, and their Director of Creativity, Jon Pearson, about what makes their organization special. You may not have heard of them, but year after year they are recognized as one of the best places to work in Omaha. As part of our field trip, Patricia arranged for us to meet a former resident, Jon Schuetz.

On March 24, 2007, Jon was in a near-fatal motorcycle accident that left him paralyzed from the chest down. He was 30 years old and single at the time, and you could say he was living the dream. But in an instant that all changed. The purpose and meaning of his life as he knew it was over.

By virtue of his relentless drive and determination, Jon took an event that 99 percent of the world would consider life ending and turned it into a new beginning.

I've spent a lot of time with Jon since that day. It's not often that you get the chance to see what a miracle looks like. I feel extremely fortunate not only to be able to interview Jon for this book, but to be able to call him a friend. I want to let Jon give his story in his own words, since he tells it better than I ever could.

I grew up in a small town, Jefferson, South Dakota, about 500 people. Mom, Dad, my brother and I. I went to Jefferson High School and was active in sports—football, cross country. They were in the same season but they allowed me to do both, so I'd go to a cross-country meet in the morning and have a football game in the evening. I also played basketball, baseball, and soccer. Went to state in cross country and track.

I moved to Sioux City when I was about 21 years old. I bought a house there. I managed a courier company there for about 7 years—Speedy Delivery; worked that job till about 2004. In that same year, there was a family reunion. About 250 of us all got together. At this particular reunion, I had a chance to catch up with my cousin Billy. He lived on Sanibel Island, just off the coast of Florida, and he asked me to come down and check out some of the businesses he owned down there. At this point I was 29. And so, spring break of 2005, I went down to Sanibel Island and spent two weeks down there just checking out the businesses he owns. He owns a tractor business, a beach rental business, bicycle, scooter, kayak rental right there on the island. I spent two weeks there that spring break, and came back to Sioux City, sold my house, and ended up moving down to Sanibel Island. I was single at the time.

So I moved down there, started working for Billy at the rental place, and lived about four blocks from the beach. In the mornings I would run on the beach when it was still dark so that, on a four-mile run, on the way back, I would get to see the sunrise. That was pretty cool for a guy from the Midwest. I did that every day for a little over a year. One day after I left work, I was heading home, riding my motorcycle, and went around a curve going a little too fast. I lost control of my motorcycle and landed against a utility box. A car stopped and asked what he should do and I said, 'Well you better call 911 because I can't feel anything below my neck.' I had trouble breathing at that time, too, but I thought I was going to be able to get back up and dust myself off. But, you know, I had to wait for the ambulance to get there.

When they got there, I was still wearing my helmet. The EMT that was there wanted to take my helmet off. I told him how to push the release button. Turns out the button had cracked when I landed, so when he pushed it, it scraped across my head and opened up a pretty good wound. They used fifteen staples taking care of that. Eventually they loaded me into an ambulance and took me to a helicopter. We flew to Lee Memorial Hospital.

The EMTs didn't really tell me much about my condition at the time. I didn't know for sure, but I knew there were some major problems because I couldn't really feel anything below my neck. They kept asking me questions, like what was my mom's name, her phone number, stuff like that. I was conscious the whole way. They took me to the emergency room and started what would end up being a two-part, four-hour surgery on my neck. They did the back surgery first: they put in two rods, two screws. Then they went in through the front and put a plate in my neck at cervical vertebrae C4, C5, C6, and C7. I had fractures so they had to fuse all those bones together.

Those surgeries were maybe six hours after the accident. So when I woke up on that same day, my mom was actually in the intensive care unit where I was. She flew down as soon as she heard what happened. I didn't know at that point where I was because she was there, and I was groggy from everything. At that point, they started talking about what was going to happen with me, and I think that scared her because they said that I had broken my neck, and it's typical for me not to have any function below that injury level. She might have to make alterations to her house and have me live with her. It was not likely that I was going to walk. That kind of thing. It was pretty emotional for her. They kept most of that from me. I had gone through that traumatic experience, and they didn't want to lay all that on me all at once, so I found out about that over time.

I spent eight days in intensive care at Lee Memorial Hospital in Fort Myers. Then they moved me to the rehab floor and I spent about four and a half weeks there. And that was just doing light therapy—I was still in the hospital bed, still had all the staples and stitches everywhere. It's weird, the only other thing I got aside from the neck injury and the wound on my head was just a little scratch on my hand.

I was starting to do some physical therapy in that first four and a half weeks after the ICU and was realizing that I didn't have a whole lot of movement in my upper body and zero in my lower body—and that was me realizing that, you know, this isn't like a broken arm and I'm not going to heal up in a few weeks.

While I was at the hospital on the rehab floor, I developed a pressure sore on my tailbone. I didn't know at the time that those could be fatal, and mine was a stage four, which is one of the most serious ones. So they had a special doctor come in and work with that.

For my mom to be able to stay in Florida with me, people at her work donated their vacation time to her. So she was able to do that. She wanted me to come back to Sioux City as soon as possible so she didn't have to rely on her coworkers to help her out. Our idea was to get me to Mercy Hospital in Sioux City and work with one of the best skin doctors there to help me with my pressure sore. The doctors in Florida didn't really want me to fly—of course, I couldn't fly at the time because I wasn't sitting upright, and there were blood pressure challenges and things like that. Maybe I was upright three or four minutes a day so I had to be laying down most of the time. The blood pressure problem was pretty serious. They would get me up for maybe 30 seconds and they'd be trying to talk to me and I wouldn't be able to answer. Most people have blood pressure problems after a spinal cord injury. I'm considered a 'C-5' for cervical vertebrae five—that's the highest level I can function at.

To get me home, we found a medevac plane service. They would come and pick me up at the hospital, take me to an airport, then take me on a plane to Sioux City's airport. That was around the middle of April. They got me back to Mercy Hospital in Sioux City, and they had to start working immediately on the pressure sore. We had to take care of that before I could really start on physical therapy. The sore was as big as two fists around and it was deep to the bone. I can remember actually a nurse turning me over before the sore developed, I remember her coming in and saying, 'Oh, we got a little red spot there. It's about the size of a dime. We really need to keep an eye on that.' Within two days it was a full-blown pressure sore. They start from the inside and work their way out and can be caused from a wrinkle in the sheet. My sensory was affected so I couldn't tell if I was uncomfortable at the time. Nothing below my neck really. Everything was pretty dull except for a little bit in my hands and arms. I had that bedsore for over a year. At its worst, I had it for probably six months.

Through this time I'm realizing that I can't put clothes on for myself or brush my teeth. Staff is doing a lot of stuff for me, and one day I just looked in the mirror and saw a shadow of myself. I was really skinny. I'd lost about 35 pounds since I got injured and I just couldn't believe that I was looking at myself. That's when I started to realize it was pretty serious and I thought, "whatever they tell me to do I'm going to work on." The next two weeks after that realization I'm just working as hard as I could, putting that determination that I had before to work for me now.

I was a pretty determined guy. I didn't let a whole lot stop me. Before the accident, I had always kept my body in shape and did a lot of workout routines and things like that. But now things were so different. I didn't know I was such a determined person until after this happened. You do take it for granted, just being able to do normal things whenever you want. You really check your intestinal fortitude after trauma like this. Throughout the rehabilitation process, I wanted to get as close to the lifestyle that I had before my injury, and I didn't want to let myself down, so that gave me drive and pushed me through to today.

Jon is a pretty modest, no-drama guy. Even though I've known him for a little while now and am familiar with his story, there are some things about it that I find nothing short of remarkable. The first is the abruptness of the change. Jon went from taking sunrise runs in the Gulf of Mexico to a yearlong struggle against a bedsore. Take a moment to strap yourself into that reality, then check your own intestinal fortitude. You might need to recalibrate the meaning of the words "tough" and "challenge" afterward.

The other remarkable thing about his story is his demeanor, his resolve, and his discipline. Jon has gone through more struggle and agony in a few years than many accumulate in an entire lifetime. Yet in all the time I've spent with him, I've never heard Jon get angry about what happened. He's never asked, Why me?, or broken down or spent any time at all on things that he wanted to do but now can't. Some people get more worked up by a bad day than Jon does talking about his life-changing injury.

We're all going to face change in our lives. When faced with change, you can't always control the outcome. But you *can* control your outlook and your attitude. If Jon Schuetz can respond in a positive way to his life-altering event, it really puts things in perspective. If *he* can do it, what's my excuse?

What is Jon doing with himself these days? Conventional wisdom would lead us to assume that since that day in March of 2007, he hasn't been able to do a whole lot. Conventional wisdom is wrong. Since then, Jon has gotten married, fathered four boys, climbed Half Dome once and El Capitan twice, goes kayaking, designed a home, re-learned to drive a car, joined a rugby team, learned to play tennis, received scuba diving certification, and has become a mentor to others with spinal-cord injuries at QLI.

As a father, Jon makes dinner most days of the week, drives the kids where they need to go, and takes them on bike rides. As a mentor on QLI's campus, Jon is a living example to other residents of how they should never set their sights any lower than they did before meeting with their own twists of fate. He teaches the basics of maneuvering into and out of wheelchairs, vehicles, beds, and other furniture. He teaches how to recover after a fall. He's there for you if you need emotional and spiritual support. And he's there to kick your butt at tennis or rugby. Speaking of rugby, Jon drives himself to practice once a week and puts three hours into it. Two times a year the team travels to tournaments all over the U.S., including Minneapolis, Denver, Milwaukee, and St. Louis. Jon received his scuba diving certification in his capacity as a mentor at QLI. He helped someone fulfill their dream while also fulfilling his own— one that he had before his own accident.

4
A Leap of Faith

It's breathtaking, isn't it? Every single one of those things listed above is a genuine achievement. Every single activity is a feat that defies all explanation. Jon's accident wasn't life ending. It was a new beginning. While talking with QLI's Director of Creativity, Jon Pearson, we broached the idea of "coping" versus "thriving." Everyone wants to thrive in life, but when we have our own figurative or literal motorcycle accident, we might wake up to a new reality in which we can no longer function like we used to. At that point, we're in a coping phase. We have to cope with the change. That's natural and necessary. But at some point, as Jon Pearson says, "Coping sounds like 'just getting by.' But if it were me in one of these chairs, I'd want to thrive. How do I thrive?" He continued by saying:

So that's what makes Jon remarkable. Just looking at the injury first of all—you could have two people with the same exact injury as Jon, a spinal cord injury. But their response from a life situation perspective could be completely different. The first of them may believe: "My life is over. What's the point? My wife could never love me like this. I'll never have children. Every goal I had is gone..." They will have the accident, go through some therapy, and truly believe that there is no point.

Someone like Jon mourns and grieves and goes through that process but, eventually, dusts himself off and says, "Well, I can't undo this. I wish I could, but I can't. I'm young and I want a life that's worth living. How do I do that? What's that look like?" It's not always a completely new path. Jon's always been a competitor. Okay, what do you like about that? It's the camaraderie, the competition, the physical aspect… Jon did a nice job of not having blinders on: "I can't play basketball anymore, so what's the point?" No, he didn't say that, he said, "Other sports are available to me. If I can't do what I did before, I'll find something new."

It's easy to talk about thriving in an environment of change, but how do you actually do it? Based on my own life experiences, and illuminated by meeting Jon and hearing about his, I will share my insights on what worked well for me. Starting from a general perspective, we can break it down into three parts: people, purpose, and culture.

PEOPLE

For Jon, as for many of us, people are the first and most important key to thriving. It starts with your parents and those who help influence and teach you in your upbringing. The environment that is constructed for you when you can't take care of yourself as a child and youth has a tremendous impact on your potential later in life, even if you think you don't remember it. For Jon, his father was absent, so his grandfather played a very important role. One of Jon's most vivid memories is of inviting his grandfather to a race he was going to run. He really respected his grandfather, and to be able to ask his grandfather to come, then perform to the best of his ability and win the race meant a lot to Jon. We also saw the true measure of his mother, as she made it down to Florida to be with him mere hours after the accident.

The other people that really make a difference are those you surround yourself with. Who makes up your inner circle? These are the people who support you in your most difficult moments and celebrate your successes, too. We've already mentioned Jon's mother, and we've already mentioned his children. But we have yet to introduce another miraculous figure in this whole story: Jon's wife, Erin.

Erin first met Jon very briefly after he had moved to Florida. He was back for the holidays around January and they were at a party together. It was just a casual meeting at a party. Sioux City, Iowa, isn't a big town, so when news of Jon's accident reached the community in 2007, Erin heard it. She said she cried and cried about it. "I thought he's too nice a guy to have that happen to," she recalls. "They didn't know then that Jon would live. It was awful."

Once Jon had returned to Sioux City, Erin started to visit him regularly. "We didn't know the extent of his injury, but we went up to the hospital and he was always in such good spirits. Even from the beginning. You would not have known the struggles he was going through because he was always happy, and glad to have company. He was excited when we would come up and visit him. I'm sure it was hard and lonely and… devastating, because his world had completely changed. So we'd play board games or watch movies. He didn't get to eat a lot in the hospital so we always found it fun to bring him different foods. We snuck some hot wings in, some Big Macs… I did not know that it would lead to a relationship. We had a lot in common— it was very easy to hang out with Jon." As Jon's recovery progressed, so did his relationship with Erin. They each became a bigger part of the other's life: she would drive to Omaha on Wednesday evenings to eat dinner and hang out, then return for a couple nights on the weekend. Erin is an elementary school teacher, and eventually Jon worked his way into her classes. "My first graders loved making him cards. They always asked about Jonny–When is Jonny getting out of the hospital? Can he come to our class and visit? When he went to QLI, he was there for seven months. When he came back home, once a week he would come into the classroom, where he would read to them, and help them with craft projects." As Jon puts it now, the beginning of their relationship was "emotionally huge" for his recovery: "It was so great to have her there while I was going through this time in my life. Just getting out and going to places, I could transfer into her car, she would break down my wheelchair and put it in her trunk. I would think to myself, 'I'm going to get into the car with my girl- friend and we're going to go somewhere. Go out on a date.'"

Jon left QLI in November of 2008 and moved back to Sioux City, living in a house with Erin. Their lives had grown together over the past year into something unique and compelling. Jon had spent every ounce of his energy at QLI toward becoming as independent as possible. Erin felt that being with Jon was part of her own higher calling in life. She could support him when necessary, and they could both provide the other with comfort and happiness. Their new life together was special, but they weren't married yet. There was just one potential bump in the road: children. For various reasons, those with spinal cord injuries often can't have children. Jon recalled that "I had a nurse at Mercy Hospital bring up children at some point. I had never really thought about it. That was a real eye opener." Obviously Jon had to live with the consequences of the accident for the rest of his life. But was Erin ready to accept the implications of a relationship with Jon and all the sacrifices that might entail? "The thing that I was worried about the most was having kids. I had to stop and think, you know, what did I want? Was it worth not being able to have a family? Or what did I want more? I just decided that Jon was such an important person in my life, and I really do love him with all my heart, that it was worth taking that chance. It would be okay if it was just the two of us."

Their first son was born in March of 2009. Now, they have four, aged six, five, three, and eight weeks. Erin's family helped Jon acquire land and build a house. Jon designed it so that he could be as independent as possible, especially in the kitchen. Jon has been surrounded by all the right people at all the right times since the moment his motorcycle slipped out from under him. His strength of will and character attracted others cut from the same cloth to help him recover and transition to a new life. Thanks to his inner circle, that new life is not one defined by talk of limitations but adventure and possibility. "From the very beginning no one really saw Jon as having limitations," recalls Erin. "He wasn't even at QLI more than a month and a half and he was getting on an airplane to go to Las Vegas because our friends were getting married. And right after he left QLI, we took another trip to Phoenix. We try to keep things as familiar as possible, and Jon was always willing to try things."

Jon agrees. "Yeah, I was always going to push it as hard as I could. Erin realized fairly quickly that we weren't just going to sit back and let the injury take over. So, together, we didn't let anything slow us down."

PURPOSE

It's often said that the tree that bends can bend in a storm and will not break. That's true enough. But if that tree doesn't have firm ground to plant its roots in, it doesn't matter how much it can bend. It's simply going to fall over. Yes, Jon's life changed completely in March of 2007. Some would describe his lifestyle in Florida as "living the dream." But if we asked him today which life is more fulfilling and rewarding, that from before the accident or after–which do you think he would choose? I think he would say that, while he enjoyed his life in Florida and Sioux City, his life's purpose was not defined. When he suffered his spinal cord injury, the "old life" slipped away from him as easily as the motorcycle. It could carry him from one place to another, it gave him a thrill to ride–but where was he heading? What was his destination?

Now, the destination has become the journey. Jon's greater purpose in life is his family, his children, and mentoring. All these things will take a lifetime of work; none of these pursuits will ever be finished. All three challenge Jon every day, bring him into contact with new people, and force him to constantly strive to be better. Erin thinks she's a better person because of Jon. She also believes that their boys will be better people because of Jon's situation: "He has made me a more kind, compassionate person. Our goal is that our boys will grow up with that same kind of heart–they'll reach out to those in need. I want them to know that they should help as many people as they can. Jon's purpose now is to inspire others. When people hear his story, or they watch him with his kids, they have to be inspired. Because he's truly amazing. The accident kicked him into high gear. He could have easily given up. You see so many people at QLI that do–or want to–and that would be so much easier. Look at the struggles that Jon faces. Getting his clothes on, getting his socks off, his shoes. You know, I'm yelling 'Why aren't we ready to go?!'" And he always says, 'I'm the fastest quadriplegic that you'll ever meet! Settle down Erin!'"

Jon's mentoring at QLI takes many forms: sports activities, demonstrations on maneuvering through life in a wheelchair, taking questions over lunch from others with spinal cord injuries, spotting someone while working out. Sports have always been a part of Jon's life, so it's no surprise that he continues to pursue them. But it's not just about amusement and recreation. Sports are often one of the most direct means of confronting the changes brought on by traumatic injury in life:

My role–I'm someone who's available to just lean on.
Most of my interactions are emotional questions that peo-

ple have. When you first get injured you don't realize it, but the emotional side is much larger than the physical stuff. A big part of it is fear. Fear of the unknown. How their lives will look. A lot of times it's, How did I meet my wife? How do I raise kids from a wheelchair? Other times it's more technical, like how I drive a car, how I do my daily routine.

Doing adaptive sports ties into their feelings and their emotional state. We're often doing activities that they did before they were injured and making the connection to now, to the fact that they're still able to do a lot—even if it takes some extra equipment. When a huge portion of your life—something you've enjoyed for many years, when that's taken away, you don't know what you're going to fill that with. You might have spent three hours a day playing guitar, playing piano, things like that, and now that's gone. Some people want to get back to doing that as soon as possible, or they don't want anything to do with it at all.

The most interesting part about the work is helping them find something to be passionate about. Whether it's something totally different from what they're used to or finding something they've always wanted to do but haven't done yet, we'll try to pool our resources here and make it happen for them.

Over the years I like to think I've encouraged people to chase what they love to do, just like this young gal wanted to scuba dive and now she's going to be certified next year. There was another young man, probably four years ago, who was passionate about music. He wanted to get back into making music and I encouraged him to do that—he was a guitar player. With his injury he was no longer able to do that. So we tried to find other ways, just to make him happy with the life he has now. He went and did some of the rugby stuff with me. We also got him out to the kayak dock down at Cunningham Lake. We had to design that dock, and figure out how that was going to work–how someone with a disability can go out and kayak if they want to.

It's an amazing feeling to be able to help somebody in a situation similar to your own–to help them achieve their short term goals, or just to be happy in life, in the moment.

What is the nature of the change in Jon's life? How do we weigh the "good" against the "bad"? Do we get the "good"–the mentoring, the family, the children–without the "bad"? In abstract, these might be difficult to answer. That's why Jon's life and example are so powerful. We don't have to wonder about it; we can look the answer right in the eye. Change is not about looking toward the past and wishing that you still had this, that, or the other– it's about being brave enough to know what you can do in the present moment. It's about having the vision to see what your capabilities *now* can lead to in the future, if only you have the determination and the inner circle to get you there.

5

Life Changing Culture

Individuals are the building blocks of organizations. Individuals with their own passions, goals, and sense of purpose. It's easy to get caught up in slogans, logos, commercials on TV, or big fancy buildings when thinking of a given organization. Conventional wisdom judges the success of a business model by how much money it generates. I'm here to tell you that without the right organizational *culture*, nothing else matters. Without a clear vision and alignment of organizational goals with your key stakeholders, will sustainable success be possible?

Jon is a force of nature, no doubt about that. But where would he be without Erin or the people at QLI? Obviously the culture there had a life-changing impact on him, and now he's giving back. He's become a part of the team. He's doing it because QLI taught him that the first thing he needed to worry about was what he wanted to do, not what he *thought* he could do.

Let's think about this for a moment. When Jon was at the hospitals in Fort Meyers, Florida and Sioux City, Iowa, the nurses and doctors were focused on two things: getting him through the immediate trauma, and preparing him for what he wouldn't be able to do for the rest of his life. These included living by himself, driving a car, cooking, having children, working, playing sports, traveling. If that's all that Jon had ever heard after the accident, where would he be today? What would he be doing?

Compare that to what happened at QLI, where it's not only about rehabilitation, but it is also about finding out how your new life is going to function most successfully. The residents–not patients–at QLI are part of a caring, supportive family. They are given hope. At the same time, they are pushed into new uncomfortable situations. One moment that surprised Jon during his stay was a staff member telling Jon, "Okay, it's time to go." "Where?" he asked. "To the grocery store. I want to see how you handle it." Or, "Hey, we're going out on a pontoon boat this weekend. Do you want to go?"

"It's a neat little community," as Jon describes it, "because there are those opportunities, those invitations. And some people are scared, and some people are at the threshold where they can try that, and some have become comfortable with doing those activities." Jon began work as a mentor at QLI about three and a half years after he himself graduated to independent living. "I had my injury and moved back to Sioux City, and then I was in contact with QLI because they like to keep up with past residents. I had been doing some outpatient therapy and QLI, it turns out, wanted to expand their mentor roles. My original capacity was going to be showing people how to do transfers into or out of their wheelchairs. It really has blossomed since then, as far as getting into every aspect of someone's life. Physical therapy and occupational therapy as well, but the recreational part is what I teamed up with Ed Armstrong on. He's QLI's Director of Adaptive Sports. When we first started we had visions of getting people out hunting and how that would look, and getting the right equipment –the bikes, the kayaks, all the adaptive sports equipment we have."

The culture of achievement and innovation–of always pushing the envelope personally and organizationally–is pervasive at QLI. It's dyed in the wool there. Everything is focused on the humanity of each and every individual in the facility, and everything *springs* from the humanity of every individual. That goes for staff and residents alike. Because there is no set "plan" for a given injury, ability level, or emotional state, every individual at every level has to be ready to pitch in and give 110%. Fittingly enough, you'll hear that message in some form or another from all levels at QLI. I had the opportunity to speak with Patricia Kearns, the CEO, recently. She spoke at length about the unique–and uniquely successful–culture at work there. "At QLI, we have an obligation to dream about what's possible rather than just accepting what the research says, or what a physician says. This is an obligation to our patients, their families, but also to our company. Innovation is the key to helping the people we serve be successful, and it's the key to keeping the doors of the company open for the long term. We try to break down barriers and create a flat system. To have a level of ownership and responsibility, to bring new ideas forward, to recognize when things aren't going well and need to be changed–that's what it is to be innovative, to be curious, to dream. It doesn't matter where you work here, whether you're the CEO, or a clinician, or if you work in housekeeping. We all have a responsibility to be innovative."

"Our primary focus is to allow people to do what

they're good at. We hire people who are passionate about learning, who have an innate curiosity. We allow people this opportunity to develop their skills and learn more. We have a lot of people who make an effort to get better at the things they're not good at, which is important. From a leadership perspective, our goal is to understand people's strengths, put them in a position to maximize those strengths, and then help them embrace people on their team who are good at all the things which they're not good at. We have a saying, 'Revel in talent.' That shows our emphasis on every member of a team appreciating the strengths of their team members. We can function better as a team than as individuals."

In this sense, QLI is the epitome of a purpose-driven organization, and Jon is a living example of the power of purpose-driven leadership. We saw earlier that when Jon started as a mentor, his original capacity was very specific: demonstrating transfers into and out of a wheelchair for residents. As he put it, the role soon "blossomed" into something far richer and impactful. No one in an office somewhere made the decision that he would eventually, for example, build a wheelchair-accessible dock and take people out on kayaks. Nor did someone in an office some-where *check his decision to do that*. If no one would have ben-efitted from it, it wouldn't have been built. The needs of the individuals dictated the potential approaches, and eventu-ally one was carried through to completion. Now it's just another tool in the toolbox to recovery and thriving. The journey itself was the destination, and now the destination has become a mile-marker for others in their own journeys.

All of this happened because QLI trusted Jon to do what was best for himself and others, and Jon was empowered by QLI to believe in all the possibilities. "Whatever he's doing, it's never just about him, or his title, or power," says Patricia. "It's about the people around him. And he's curious: he wants to know more, he wants to do more, and he's not afraid of failure. He inspires other people to succeed."

Jon isn't afraid of failure. QLI isn't afraid of failure either, because there is no predefined definition of "success" other than getting people back on-track to living meaningful lives–which is exactly what Jon is working toward. The goals and needs of the "client" and the company in this case are completely codependent. They share the same incentives. With the needs of the company so clearly defined by the needs of the people who seek it out, it's no surprise that QLI has been voted the best place to work in Omaha, Nebraska, five separate times.

By all accounts, it's an amazing place to live, too. People hear "rehabilitation center" and the image that pops into their head is a negative one. Injury, struggle, disability, compromise. But walk the halls and you'll soon find yourself in a hub of activity and energy. Residents live together a bit like roommates, with both private and shared spaces. The residents are making plans, interacting with each other, heading out the door to the nearest park. It's a powerful blend of deep personal introspection translated into community action. At some point you might need to walk up to someone and ask if they live there or work there. And in the end, whichever the case, it's not a meaningful distinction anyway.

Jon Pearson, QLI's Director of Creativity, really drove the point home for me with a story.

Thinking a little bit about your business–your customers choose to be there. Right? But at QLI, the customers don't choose to be here. No one asks for this to happen. They just want to go back to their life. We have the most reluctant customers in the world! Yet you come to this place and it's positive, it's energetic, it's upbeat. I've had residents–I'm picturing a young gal, one day she was crying outside my office door. I said, "What's going on?" She said, "Today's my last day. I'm excited to go home, but I'm going to miss this place." Who cries when they leave the hospital? People are crying when they leave here. That's powerful.

If you're a financial company, and you don't have that culture–and we can do that here with people who are broken, whose families are in turmoil? What's your excuse? I don't want to hear that you can't do it, that you don't have the time or resources. If we can do it here, you can do it anywhere.

By the same token, you've mentioned purpose. We have a mission here that other places don't have. Most people want to be a part of something bigger than themselves, and QLI has that built in.

I've talked to a lot of business owners and managers in my lifetime. I've read a lot of leadership books and sat through many conferences. But Patricia and QLI truly are unique and stand out from the crowd. Unlike most CEOs, the longer you talk to Patricia, the more blurred the boundary between "employee" and "client" becomes. "We set a culture that is focused on growth and opportunity, that's focused on not only the individuals we serve but the staff as well. I definitely think part of getting connected to the purpose of the company is seeing that you can have a significant impact on the lives and the families of those who we are serving. That's the first step in developing a healthy culture." QLI doesn't just talk the talk when it comes to purpose-driven leadership. They also walk the walk.

The seriousness of its work requires that QLI put a lot of thought into its hiring and training processes. There's just so much at stake. Patricia put it to me this way:

What we do is hard work. We're working with people whose path in life has been completely changed. They've been devastated. They can't physically function the same way—and maybe cognitively, emotionally too things have changed. So we're trying to put a really complex treatment program together and plan a new path in life for that person. That requires our teams to be able to embrace conflict.

That's a complex skill: managing healthy intellectual conflict. Not everybody is cut out for that. Our team members have to be able to challenge each other. We have a saying here: "Stupid idea; let's have lunch." We have to have intellectual conflict—not personal—in order to push each other toward the very best ideas and the very best outcomes.

There is a risk, though, in that intellectual conflict can quickly turn into personal conflict. So healthy conflict is a skill that we actively teach here. And new people coming in, they have to be open to new learning to really be able to embrace this concept, this skill set, and use it to contribute.

When Jon Pearson was hired, he taught a course about coping. Intellectually, he understood the need for the course. When confronted with a big change, people need to know how to cope. But it felt wrong to him. He felt that the class should be about thriving, about productively dealing with change:

How do you respond to change? We're talking about Jon because he responded to one of the biggest life changes any of us could ever have thrown our way with grace and fortitude. That may make you feel good, what I've just said. But how do you do it? There are a lot of elements. Shaping your attitude. Who do you surround yourself with? How do you talk to yourself? What are your thought processes?

I've always said the biggest indicator of how someone's going to respond to a catastrophic injury is how they responded to adversity in the past. So Jon was probably someone who responded really well. That doesn't mean you can't learn good ways to respond.

There's a connection to business here, right? The businesses that can change are the ones that are still around, are the ones that thrive. The others have to shut their doors or sell to someone who knows better. Or what about the businesses that are just coping with some sort of change? Will they survive the next hit?

**

In the financial services business, our clients choose us. They make the final call as to whether they want to do business with us. The residents at QLI didn't choose. At best, they reluctantly ended up there. They didn't choose the life they're now leading.

But it's not a dark, depressing place. Just the opposite. It's vibrant, uplifting, happy. Not because of the buildings and grounds, but because of the people. They've built a culture of people who buy into the mission—people who truly believe in it.

The residents at QLI achieve great things. Truly great things. *None of them chose to be there.* What's their secret? The culture that QLI has cultivated demands those results—it demands that you believe in yourself and take the reins of your own destiny, even if the broader culture—conventional wisdom and perceptions—is always telling you it's impossible. "You can't walk. That means you can't drive, because you need fully functioning legs to drive a car. If you can't drive, you can't get groceries, or go to the doctor by yourself, or pick your kids up from school or daycare."

"You can't play rugby! You're a paraplegic!" Living independently, how?

"I know you had a dream of scuba diving. But after the accident…"

At QLI these aren't excuses. They're hardships, admittedly. Nothing is sugarcoated. But expectations are not lowered because the circumstances have changed. Taking up photography in a wheelchair *is* different from "the norm." That's okay. It doesn't mean you have to change the dream. Instead, change the journey to reach it.

When great leaders see hardship, they see opportunity. Rather than fear change, they embrace it. As a result, the teams that they lead are always looking to play to their strengths, to motivate themselves.

Why is leaving a legacy important? I've thought a lot

about that. Jon has helped me understand the answer to that question. I met Jon on November 5, 2015. It's only been a few months but already I'm a better husband, father, grandfather today because of the blessing he is in my life. It's an honor to call him a friend. He had to redefine his purpose after a motorcycle accident left him paralyzed from the chest down. He was 30 years old, single, living on an island in Florida. You could say that he was living the dream. But in an instant that all changed. The meaning and purpose of his life was over.

And then what?

His relentless purpose and inner drive kicked in. He was dealing with a different body, a body that many thought was less capable than before. This is what everyone focused on. But the most profound changes were happening inside, where no one could see. And once Jon was up, once Jon was over that bedsore and throwing himself into therapy, it became obvious that he was indeed dealing with a different set of capabilities. Whereas before he was like most of the rest of us, going through the motions, getting by, marking time. But now, faced with the most important decision of his life, to cope and just get by or to thrive?

The accident became his instrument, his voice. The thing that brought new purpose and meaning to his life.

The accident was the first turning point in his life. It led to all the rest—and if you asked him now, Jon would say that all of the meaningful decisions he's made so far in life have come *after* the accident. After the event that most told him would *end* his life as we all understand the term. Meeting his wife Erin. Having four boys. Designing and building a house. Working as a mentor and coach to other spinal cord patients, helping them find purpose and meaning.

The legacy of leadership, the daily example that his life is for his boys. Don't let your circumstances change your view of what's possible. Yes, Jon is paralyzed. Yes, Jon is in a wheelchair. But he refuses to let that change what he thinks is possible. It's why he joined a wheelchair rugby team in Omaha. It's why he took on the challenge of becoming certified to scuba dive. It's why he learned to drive—so he could pick up his boys three days a week from school. It's why he commutes 85 miles each way, two days a week, to mentor and coach spinal cord patients. To give them hope, to share his story, and to be the best role model and leader that he can be.

None of us knows what's around the next corner. Jon certainly didn't think his life would play out as it has. But when you get to know Jon, you quickly learn that he considers himself to be one lucky guy.

So the key here is no matter what you're facing in life, don't let it limit what you think is possible. Use your legacy of leadership to define how you will be remembered. After all, isn't it the people we lead, the people we care about and love that matter most?

So I challenge everyone to think about the legacy they're going to leave. What's the model you present day in and day out? How will you choose to be remembered? How will you live on in others?

***

As our friendship has grown, I have shared with Jon when we are together I don't even see the wheelchair, I don't see the disability and challenges he has to deal with on a daily basis. What I see is a passionate, purpose driven leader who had to get past the "Why?" before dealing with "How?" By this I mean he had to answer, "Why did this happen to me?" Then he was able to move on to thinking about *how* he wants to be remembered, and what he wants his legacy to be.

A chance meeting with Jon on November 5th helped me define why leaving a legacy is so important to me. Through the lens of Jon I was able to see the world from an entirely different perspective. To not let the challenges we all face in life define us, but to use them to find greater purpose and meaning and to really think about the difference and legacy we want to leave.

Section 3
Capstones

6

DEFINING MOMENTS

Up until now I've been giving you the framework, which I feel contributed greatly to some of the successes I've had in my professional career. As I think back, there were several instances, events, situations that really stand out, that began to shape and mold me, first as an athlete and then as a young professional, and then a husband, a father, a grandfather. And those things that I call on, that I think about as I reflect back on my life at this point, they are defining moments.

One of those defining moments is a story about my brother. We were thick as thieves growing up. We supported each other 100 percent of the time in everything, and especially in sports. My brother Gary is 6½ years younger than me and it seems like only yesterday that I was hitting ground balls to him in the backyard or throwing footballs that he would have to go horizontal in order to catch. He only had one speed and it was all out. Because of our age difference he looked at me not only as his older brother but his coach too. One of those coaching moments occurred when he was 12 years old and preparing to compete in an AAU sanctioned track meet. I was right there with him up until the moment he was called to the starting line. As I laced up his shoes, I heard a voice next to me. "Hey." We looked up. A coach and another runner sat across from us, in the same situation as us. The coach lacing up the shoes of the other participant. The coach grinned and said, "My runner has never been beat." My brother was nervous before races, very worked up–and I recall seeing his chin sag a little. I quickly replied, "Not until today." It was a very simple statement but it was very profound. It was a confidence shot in the arm when he needed it most. My brother still talks about that moment to this day. What transpired next was my brother setting a national age group record in the 880 yard run that stood for many years.

I think back to my high school days, being part of a winning team, having teammates, believing in each other, setting goals, that, each year, became bigger than the goals we had from the previous year.

Another defining moment was losing my Dad at such a young age. I think back on the decisions, the actions, all the things we had to put in motion, that were so unexpected. You don't expect to lose a parent at the age of 51. Looking back, I feel blessed and fortunate to have had the time I had with my Dad. But what I wouldn't give for another year, 5 years, 10 years with him. I regret the fact he didn't get to see his seven grandchildren grow up to be truly special people. What joy and happiness they would have brought to his life. We all have challenges; we all have obstacles we need to overcome. Hopefully these challenges will help us have a better understanding that life is precious, not to be taken for granted, and to have a greater appreciation for the things that matter most.

The first opportunity to qualify for the US Olympic Marathon Trials of 1980 was in the 1979 Boston Marathon. What made that so difficult was the fact that it was not only a marathon, but I was running that marathon just a few days after losing my dad. And it's not a 6 mile run around the track, it's a 26.2 mile event. You have to be in the game not only physically, but mentally as well over an extended period of time. You're out there for over two hours competing with many of the best runners in the world. This was another defining moment for me: the defining moment of having my brother in the finish area and the enormity of making that happen. If you've ever been to one of these large events, the security makes it next to impossible to get into the finish area. But my brother had a will to be there for me. That was a defining moment, the ability to mentally be in the game for an extended period of time after the passing of my Dad. I look back upon the year following that, competing in the US Olympic Trials and the dedication it took. Overall I had to set a goal, prepare, a lot of it's the journey as you prepare for an event like that. I had to sit down and plan, put my strategy together including my training regimen, and then have the discipline to stick with it. Life is not unlike a marathon. You must learn to enjoy the journey as you're keeping your eye on your goals. In life, in business, in athletics–whatever your passion is, it's the journey and being able to enjoy it. If its only about the destination how do you stay the course?

In life, we have to find those things that we're truly passionate about. My passion was running.

My defining moments (the National Cross Country Championships, my NCAA National Track Championship, the Olympic Marathon Trials) prepared me for my professional career. But at the time, when I was lacing up my running shoes, listening to coach Greeno, going to bed early–at the time, while I was making sacrifices and training, I wasn't thinking about my future professional career. Or defining moments. Or even discipline, at least not as an abstract principle. This was my life transformed into pure discipline in the original sense of the word, of getting rid of all superfluous elements. Enter into the crucible of your own passion and hold yourself there. If you can do this and see past the pain to the tooth-gritting pleasure of your inner drive, you have started down a path that only you can take, and only you can keep open by dedication to your own individual passion.

When you have found your own path and walked it for a time, only then can you help others find theirs and shepherd them along. Virtues like finding strengths, instilling confidence when it flags, belief in the face of setbacks or failures, looking toward the higher purpose of the group while developing the individuals within it–these are things, which you must embrace and acquire first within yourself. These are the instincts and talents that all great leaders have.

Entering the Financial Services business in 1981, I brought with me some experiences, which some people my age hadn't had. Up until that point, running had been my passion, whatever my job at the time. My own interests led me to work for the FBI and the Nebraska Attorney General's Office, but I never found a sense of purpose there. The overwhelming sense of purpose was obviously running, and the goal of making it to the Olympics, but being married and thinking about a family changed all that.

And just like you have done in your life, or are doing right now, I was looking for a way to combine a sense of purpose with my passion; I was looking for an answer to the question "Why?"

Life is strange that way. For the thing that truly helped me find a sense of purpose and an outlet for my passion in the early stages of my life was death. First, the death of my father. Then, a year after that, my wife's mother succumbed to cancer after a four-year struggle. And, after that, when you think you've been through real tragedy, my wife's 30 year old sister was taken by a debilitating disease.

We all look for stability in life. We all look for meaning and order. But for those of us who have encountered it, death is really the one thing in life that can't be argued with. Death is the appearance of a sudden hole in what you had previously thought to be a sound and enduring part of your reality. Its your faith, family, and close friends that help you get through these times of uncertainly. That and your own inner strength.

I was looking for something that I could wrap my arms around and believe in, something that combined passion and purpose. I didn't understand what I was getting into at the very start, but I knew I believed in the mission and the difference life insurance can make in the lives of the people it touches. Through the reality of my own family situation, it was easy to find conviction for being in the life insurance business. I had it from day one. My personal experiences changed my view and gave me a different perspective. This certainly played a big part in my early success. I wanted to make sure the people I was serving in this wonderful profession had a plan, had a financial roadmap to follow, and had something in place so that in the event they died or became disabled, their family would be taken care of. What really drove me from the very beginning we're the defining moments that I had prior to entering the business. When I began my career, I walked through the front door in 1981 with the belief and conviction that I was serving others through my work.

I truly believe we all need to find our path in life, our true calling if you will. My path into the insurance and financial services industry was not as direct as it may seem. Even though my family experienced first hand the events that unfold after the death of a family member, this did not motivate me to seek out a career selling life insurance. It was a call from a stranger that introduced me to a profession I never imagined myself being in. It was after the results of a local road race hit the sports page, where I was mentioned in the article, that I got the call. Back then, everyone was in the phone book, there were no Do Not Call lists, it was easy to look up someone's number and dial the phone. It was the call that changed my life. It was the manager of the Principal Financial Group Office wanting to know if I would be open to having lunch. He had a career opportunity he wanted to discuss with me. There was no way he could have known that I was actively looking to make a career change. A chance call and a lunch opened up a world that I never would have pursued on my own. In a way the business found me. Maybe fate had something to do with it. After losing my Dad and Mother-in-Law in just over a year's time, I found myself drawn to the career. And it fit me.

John Kennedy once said, "Effort and courage are not enough without purpose and direction." I found my purpose in the life insurance business. My own unique answer to the question why. As I began my career I found it easy to answer that question. I'm sure some of what my family experienced helped bring clarity to the answer. I recall vividly my early days in the business and how excited I was to get to work; to help individuals and families put plans in place so the things in life they care most about are protected. Each day I got to help and serve those I cared most about and truly make a difference. Who couldn't get excited about that? When you find your purpose and then stack passion on top of it you can move mountains. My goal was to work with everyone. And I was naive enough to think that everyone I approached would want to work with me. If only it was that easy.

It wasn't long before the calls and appointments started to get more difficult to make. In the financial services business, we call it the sophomore slump. What really helped me early on was my natural market. And this was developed through my running career and the name recognition I had in our local community. And I used this natural market to launch my career. But the one thing I realized which contributed greatly to the success I had, was this: if I could not create value and differentiate myself, set myself apart from my competition, I would soon run out of people to call on. I had belief and conviction from day one, I had a natural market from day one, and very quickly I developed a referral mindset.

I was committed to making referred lead prospecting

part of my day-to-day activity. I knew that if I had a process, believed in what I was doing, and created value for those I was serving they would help me. The key is the process or plan. Referrals won't just happen because you do a good job. You have to be proactive and ask. My goal was to have clients believe so much in the experience, they would be intentional about referring me. They would go out of their way to advocate for me. Embracing this early in my career, the importance of referrals and professional recommendations, and truly believing it, was one of the greatest contributors to the success I had.

My own beginning illustrates these ideas. My recruitment occurred because someone took a chance. For whatever reason, they guessed that my sports pedigree could translate into a sales position. One chance call led to an opportunity to serve others. Over the course of my career, I recruited dozens of people, and some have gone on to recruit as well.

If education and training are the engine, prospecting is the gasoline. Without qualified prospects to call on, the best trained and educated financial advisors struggle. Most advisors leave the business not because of poor training or poor products–they leave simply because they couldn't get in front of enough qualified prospects on a consistent basis. Conceptually, it's a pretty simple business. Execution-wise, it's one of the toughest there is. Learning the importance of positioning yourself for referrals and understanding that prospecting is not part of the time, but all the time, contributed greatly to some of my early successes.

7

MENTORSHIP– A TURNING POINT

My first professional fork in the road occurred about two years into my career when my manager approached me about coming into management. Like most great managers do. They take their best advisors and convince them a career in management is for them. Until approached, this wasn't even on my radar screen. I was working hard to build my individual practice and things were going well. But I was intrigued enough to listen. And the story was compelling. It went something like this. Cliff you have belief and conviction for what you are doing. And you are making a difference one client at a time. A career in management will give you the opportunity to exponentially multiple your efforts and impact many more through a career in leadership. Rather than selling one policy or one plan you will be selling the career opportunity. You will be giving others the opportunity you were given, and then working to develop, manage, and lead them. And what sounded too good to be true was, I didn't have to give up the clients I had worked so hard my first two years to obtain.

So the right fork I took and I entered management. Back then, there wasn't a lot of management training. You were basically thrown into the deep end of the pool and left to figure a lot of it out on your own. Welcome to Management 101. For me, the natural pull of gravity was back to serving clients and prospecting for new ones. It's what I knew and it's what I was good at. I found out quickly wearing two hats was going to be challenging. It's a full time job to build a financial services practice and it's a full time job to recruit, train, and develop young advisors. I did the latter poorly my first full year in management.

Fortunately, I had the foundation of my running career to fall back on. One of the things my running career taught me was to do everything you can to put yourself in the best position to win. My training did this for me. I drew on the faith I had in my training, to give myself the confidence I needed to compete at a high level. I applied the same discipline to my professional career. To put myself in a position to excel, I had to embrace the training and educational aspects of the business. This required a lot of commitment and study. If you want something badly enough, you just do what is necessary.

But individuals can only do so much on their own. The real magic in any organization occurs when people work together. Just when I was really struggling with the two aspects of my position, I met the most important professional mentor of my career. I was attending our national management conference in Des Moines at the beginning of my second year in management. This meeting was attended by all field leadership from across the country. During this meeting, I was introduced to Frank Kintzle, a successful Hall of Fame Manager from Cedar Rapids, Iowa. In my financial services career, I've had the honor and privilege to work with, be mentored by, and to observe many great leaders. Frank was the first and most important mentor I had in my professional career. He took me under his wing when I was a young manager and modeled for me what purpose-driven, servant leadership is all about. Frank would tell me, it's never about you and always about the organization. If you put the best interests of those you are leading ahead of your own, good things will happen. This was the beginning of what has now become a 36-year professional as well as personal relationship.

Over the years we attended countless company meetings together. We formed a Study Group with other Principal Managers and would meet quarterly. We talked on the phone and communicated on a regular basis. I'm not sure where my career in management would have gone without the early influence of Frank. One of the things I remember, and he would chuckle about, is asking him how much sleep he needed. My routine was to always get an early morning workout in at the hotel health club when we were attending company meetings. I would get off the elevator and walk through the lobby heading for the workout facility. And there was Frank, dressed for the day having a cup of coffee and reading the Wall Street Journal. This was at 6:00 or 6:30 in the morning. I'd say, Frank, the meetings don't start till 8:00. He would always say to beat the competition you have to get up before the competition and outwork them. To this day, Frank is one of the hardest working guys I've ever met. One of the things he shared with me was the importance of building a winning culture. He said one of the secrets to achieving unparalleled success is to build a culture based on mutual respect and trust. It's one of the lessons that really stuck with me, and as I look back it's one of the most important things that contributed to the success I enjoyed. Frank was an encourager. I could always count on getting a note or a call from Frank. As a young manager, I can't tell you how much that meant to me.

As my management and leadership career advanced, I called on the lessons and experiences I had working with my mentor often and they served me well. Regardless of where you are in your leadership journey, it's important for you to embrace mentorship. And the reasons are many. First, it's your opportunity to give back and make a difference in the professional life of a young advisor or manager. You can impart great wisdom from your years of experience, but each time I had the chance to mentor someone I learned as much from them. They brought greater purpose and meaning to my life. And great pride and satisfaction comes from seeing the person you are mentoring grow. Seeing another person grow by taking a genuine interest in them and giving of your time is a true act of servant leadership. Another benefit I found as a result of being a mentor is the long-term relationship and friendship that develops as a result.

Nearly every successful person in business or in life can point to at least one person who was there for them at a critical time and made a major difference. Frank was that person for me. He led by example and modeled for me what true mentorship looked like. Over the years I made it a point to serve others as a mentor. Many were emerging leaders, just getting stated in their management career, and I did this in an effort to give back to an industry that has been so good to me and my family. The ironic thing, and the outcome each time I had the opportunity to serve as a mentor, is I learned as much from them and I continued to grow through the lens of the emerging leaders I was mentoring.

My life story was shaped by so many defining moments, and the opportunity to have Frank Kintzle as my mentor was yet another one. As I think back on the leadership meeting in Des Moines and Frank's mentorship, they were turning points for me in my leadership journey. I think back now on so many lessons I learned from my Dad about leadership. From a formal education perspective he had a high school education. But he was a man of great wisdom and intellect. People followed him and had confidence in him as a leader. And the reasons were many. It started with his decision making and commitment to the desired outcome or result he wanted. Much success comes from having the confidence to make what we feel are the right decisions and having good judgment. My Dad built his leadership career on having good judgment and making sound personal as well as professional decisions. And it was the decisions he made along the way, not the conditions he grew up in, that determined the success and happiness he enjoyed.

One simple leadership lesson I learned from Dad was this, I happened to be home from college when my Mom received a phone call from Dad. I was listening to one side of the conversation and when my Mom hung up the phone I asked what that was all about. Mom proceeded to tell me that Dad had one of the State Patrol Troopers come to his office and tell him he was sure he saw a UFO while he was on duty the night before. Dad listened intently as he always did to what the trooper had to say. And then Mom went on to tell me Dad came up with a quick solution to the troopers sighting. And I said, what was that. Mom replied, Dad moved him to the day shift. I chuckle about that now, but how brilliant is that. Rather than convince the trooper he didn't see a UFO, the answer was to just move him to the day shift. The leadership lesson here is, there are times when we are searching for the complex answer to a problem or challenge we are facing, and the answer is actually pretty simple and not complex at all.

There's a great quote by Helen Keller, "Life is either a daring adventure or nothing." Isn't a daring adventure what we all seek in life, to enjoy the journey as we pursue life with passion and purpose. Well, theres a lot in life that is out of our control, but one thing we are in control of are the decisions we make and the happiness we choose to enjoy. There are so many things we can all accomplish in life if we decide what it is we are truly committed to achieving and the price we are willing to pay to go after it.

I also called on lessons learned in athletics. In high school I competed in a variety of sports but running was the one I had great passion for. So I came to the realization I could continue to play multiple sports and be average, or I could pursue the one I had the most talent for and excel. It served me well in athletics and it served me well as I embarked on my career in management and leadership.

From that point forward I was committed to a career of serving others. We all have people and experiences in our lives that shape and mold us. For me the influence of my Grandpa, my parents, my coaches and mentors, all played a role and helped shape the leader I would ultimately become.

There's a great quote by Howard Schultz, CEO of Starbucks: "The reservoir of all my life experiences shaped me as a person and a leader." This was certainly true for me. All my life experiences and defining moments became my guideposts as the world of management and leadership began to open up for me. I began to read and study the writings and teachings of great leaders and teachers, people like Zig Ziglar, Brian Tracy, and Denis Waitley. I would listen to audio tapes and attend seminars and workshops in an effort to sharpen my management and leadership skills. I spent time studying and learning from some of the industry heavyweights like Norm Levine, Phil Richards, and Harry Hoopis. As I would read their books and listen to them, it was like they were speaking to me. Through the teachings and lessons of many, I started to realize management and leadership are not the same. There's truly an art and a science to leadership and management. Let's compare and contrast what I feel some of the differences are:

LEADERSHIP

1. Leadership is not defined by your title. It's an activity, not a position
2. Leaders inspire and they influence

3. Leaders cast the vision for the organization
4. Leaders believe in people development
5. Leaders are very strategic in their thinking
6. Leaders believe in consistent execution
7. Leaders understand the importance of delegation and staying out of the weeds

MANAGEMENT

1. Managers administer and supervise
2. Managers plan and set goals for the organization
3. Managers set policy and procedures
4. Managers have a short term view
5. Managers focus on skill development

It's really managements job to look for skills and develop those skills, where leadership is focused on identifying talent. Managers spend time defining steps, and leaders define outcomes. Managers are focused on fixing weaknesses, leadership focuses on developing strengths. It's management's job to focus on building competencies, and it's the leadership that casts the vision and inspires. Management is more about seeking stability and control, and leaders are more creative in their thinking. Great leaders have passion and purpose; they can answer the question why. This is what draws people to them. They know where they want to take their organizations and their purpose is the connection that draws people together. The belief and buy-in from the team is essential for organizational goals and objectives to be achieved.

Leaders dream about what is possible. Creating a compelling vision and then articulating it so people want to follow is what great leaders do. They understand the direction the organization needs to be headed. They understand this is their responsibility. But they also understand it's important to invite others within the organization to have a voice. Purpose and vision put a frame around the why. All the colors inside the frame begin to come to life and take shape with purpose and vision. Vision lights the path and creates the walkway for others in the organization to follow. People are empowered by a vision they believe in, and they are motivated and excited by it. I've never seen an organization achieve great things by following a fuzzy vision.

Another thing great leaders have in common is they keep their egos in check. Leadership has to be about helping others get what they want. Not just professionally but personally as well. They take a genuine interest in the lives of those they serve. Inside and outside of work, they are value driven, and at their core, are persons of great integrity and character. In his book "Discover Your True North," Bill George talks about authentic leadership. He says, "authentic leaders align people around a shared purpose and values, and empower them to lead authentically to create value for all stakeholders. Authentic leaders are true to themselves and to what they believe. They engender trust and develop genuine connections with others. Because people trust them, authentic leaders are able to motivate them to achieve high levels of performance. Rather than letting the expectations of others guide them, they are their own persons and go their own ways. As servant leaders, they are more concerned about serving people than about their own success or recognition." At its core, what Bill George is talking about is that today's leaders are purpose driven, they can answer the question why, and they consistently put the needs of those they are leading ahead of their own self interests.

8

BUILDING BRIDGES OR BUILDING WALLS

As a leader, are you building bridges or are you building walls within your organization? Purpose driven leaders are constantly working to build bridges with the people they manage and lead. During my 35 years in leadership, I worked hard to make sure our culture was something everyone was proud of. I wanted everyone associated with us to not only think but feel that it was a special place to work. People want to be a part of a caring organization where mutual respect and trust exist. I truly believe you connect the dots through culture. So keeping your finger on the pulse of culture within your organization is what strong leaders do. Remember, culture is what they say it is, not what you say it is.

A way that you can keep this in check is to ask yourself this question, What kind of organization do I want to lead? Am I proud of where we stand today? Equally important is to ask your advisors and staff what kind of organization they want to be a part of. You want the two to align as closely as possible. If your philosophies, beliefs, and standards align with your people, you are well on your way to building a culture winners aspire to be a part of. As a leader, if you're not sure where you are from a culture perspective, send out a culture quiz with a series of questions. For the most part, people will tell you how they feel. As a leader, don't be afraid of the feedback you might get back. Wouldn't you rather know? The feedback will give you the opportunity to benchmark your culture and, if necessary, make changes to improve it. I can't overemphasize the importance of this. You must always strive to build a culture based on mutual respect and trust. It was something we never took for granted, something we worked on everyday.

Thinking back to my high school and college track and cross country teams, I now know how blessed I was to be a part of something special. We had great team culture and chemistry. We had mutual respect and trust. And I will take it one step further, we had genuine love in our heart for our teammates. We were there for each other and our bond was strong. A big part of this was the environment our coaches created. An environment where we trusted our coaches and we trusted each other. It's one five-letter word, trust, but without it nothing sustainable will be possible. It's what separates great teams from good ones. The one common thread that runs throughout, being an individual, or team, or business that can be trusted. So whether trust is high or low will have either a positive or negative impact on every activity and dimension within a relationship, team, or organization. Jim Burke, former Chairman and CEO of Johnson and Johnson, said, "You can't have success without trust. The word trust embodies almost everything you can strive for that will help you to succeed. You tell me any human relationship that works without trust, whether it is a marriage or a friendship or a social interaction; in the long run, the same thing is true about business, especially businesses that deal with the public."

One of the great possibility thinkers of our time is Stephen M. R. Covey. I drew much from his leadership lessons and writings. During my career I had the opportunity to hear him speak on multiple occasions. He talked often about the 13 behaviors of high trust leaders that I tried to follow in my own career. Five are character based, five are competency based, and three have elements of both.

The character behaviors are:

1. Be honest and tell the truth.
2. Demonstrate respect. Genuinely care for others
3. Create transparency. Don't have hidden agendas, don't hide information.
4. Right wrongs.
5. Show loyalty. Give credit to others, speak about people as if they're present.

The competency behaviors:

1. Deliver results. Establish a track record of results. Get things done.
2. Get better. Continuously improve; be a constant learner.
3. Confront reality. Take issues head on and address the tough stuff.
4. Clarify expectations. Disclose and reveal expectations and validate them.
5. Practice accountability. Hold yourself and others accountable.

The three that have elements of both:

1. Listen first. Listen before you speak.
2. Keep commitments.
3. Trust. Extend trust abundantly to those who have earned it, and extend trust conditionally to those who are earning it."

Can you imagine the heights you and your organization can soar if you embrace the 13 behaviors? If developed and leveraged, they have the potential to create unparalleled success within every aspect and dimension of your life. Look at them closely, ask yourself, how am I doing? What behaviors can I improve on? It's up to you, you are in control. How exciting is that?

I'd like to share a story where the 13 behaviors really come to life. It's a story about being honest and setting clear expectations. It's a story about transparency of communication, respect and loyalty. It's a story about confronting the reality of the situation and clarifying expectations. And most important it's a story about keeping commitments and abundant trust. And it's a true story about the 2014-2015 Duke basketball team.

I have to admit I've never been a huge fan of Duke basketball, but I am a huge fan of Coach K, Mike Krzyzewski. Coach K's teams always seem to find a connection to something bigger than basketball. The incredible story of Duke's 2014-2015 season appeared in the September 2015 issue of *Success* magazine and was written by my good friend Don Yaeger. The season started with great promise and, as was customary for Duke, they set their sights on

being national champions, cutting down the nets the first
Monday in April. But what happened in January was
uncharacteristic. In fact it had never happened in Coach
K's 35 year coaching the Duke team. He had to dismiss a
player for disciplinary reasons. They then dropped three
out of their next six games. And what made matters worse,
they had some players go down to season ending injuries.
What appeared to be a championship caliber team was
now on the brink.

Coach K called a team meeting and shared with the
team they were down to eight players. 'It's all we have, and
it's all we need' was his message. One by one, he went
around the room reminding each player why they were
special, why now more than ever before they all needed to
raise their game. And then he declared the goal of being
national champions had not changed.

I'm sure you could have heard a pin drop in that locker
room. As a result of that team meeting, the team got back
on track. And wouldn't you know it, just before the NCAA
Tournament, associate head coach Jeff Capel had an idea
which was kept quiet from the public. Coach K called
another team meeting and he brought out a ball and marker. He said, we are going to have this ball with us as we
make our way through the tournament. We would like for
you to write the names of the people who have made it
possible for you to be here, the people who have been
there for you and supported you. Then coach K said, we
are going to take the ball with us everywhere we go but we
won't tell the public. Coach K began by writing seven
names on the ball—his wife and three daughters, his high

school coach, a close friend, and his priest when he was growing up in Chicago. Then he called on each player to write their names on the ball. Then he said, after we win the championship and cut down the nets we are going to send an autographed ball and a letter to each name on the ball and tell them how they helped carry us through the tournament; that they were with us every step of the way. The players started carrying the ball around–to team meals, on the plane, at practices, in the locker room. Some of the guys slept with it. The ball sat on the bench as they began their march through the tournament. Coach K said it was a powerful reminder of how many people were responsible for their being in that moment. Well, the rest is history. Duke went on to beat the University of Wisconsin in the final game to fulfill a dream, a goal they set at the beginning of the season.

Why has Mike Krzyzewski been successful his entire coaching career? I believe it's because he practices the 13 behaviors of high trust leaders. He recruits kids with character that fit the Duke culture. He sets high expectations and holds his players accountable. Coach K says, "the most incredibly interesting thing about being a leader is what adjustments you make and how you make them while keeping your core principles alive and well."

As you continue your leadership journey, be mindful of the 13 behaviors of high trust leaders. Work hard to develop a culture where mutual respect and trust exist, where openness and transparency of communication are practiced, and where expectations are clearly communicated.

When you do, magical things will begin to happen in the professional as well as personal lives of those you are serving.

9

POSSIBILITY THINKING– A SLIGHT EDGE

I've had the privilege and opportunity to work with great people in my 36 professional career. There are several things that stand out when I think about successful people, and the first is they view themselves as successful. They think constantly in terms of: I can, I will, and I am. "I'll try" is not part of their vocabulary. They are not just open to new learning, they are aggressive in their pursuit of it. Change is something they embrace, and they are constantly looking at ways to close the gap between their performance and their potential. Winners and leaders in life use adversity as fuel. It's a lot easier to achieve success when things are comfortable. But what happens when things get turned upside down. Its during these times that winners use the adversity they are facing as fuel to take them to a place they wouldn't otherwise go. They always keep the goal out in front of them, and they visualize victory. And maybe the most important they are possibility thinkers. Ask yourself this question, Am I doing everything I can to incorporate possibility thinking into my day to day life?

One of the great possibility thinkers of our time was New York City Mayor Rudy Giuliani. In the hours following the tragic events of 9/11 when the city of New York was turned upside down, the Mayor was able to give the people of New York a sense of confidence when it was desperately needed most. In the days following he was asked to give some perspective, and what he said was, "I was incredibly proud of the people of New York, there was no chaos, but they were frightened and concerned, and I knew they needed to hear from my heart the direction we were going." Sixteen hours after the planes struck the buildings when he returned home to get some rest, rather than sleeping he picked up and read several chapters of a World War II autobiography, about how Winston Churchill helped his people see the possibilities and keep going. Isn't it ironic, all these years later Mayor Giuliani did the same for the citizens of New York? As I thought about this it struck me, the profession I've been so passionate about, is all about helping our clients, helping those we serve see the possibilities and keep going. Whether it's the loss of a loved one, the loss of income due to a disability, or the prospects of living an uncertain retirement because of limited income. These are the times our clients come to us frightened and concerned. And it's during these times they want to know one thing. Am I going to be ok, is my family going to be ok, will my business survive? What an incredible opportunity, but more important than the opportunity, it's the obligation we have to do our jobs to the very best of our ability and serve our clients well. Isn't it amazing the power that comes from being a possibility thinker?

A great sports story about the power of possibility thinking was witnessed by millions of people who saw the greatest comeback in NBA history when the Cleveland Cavaliers, down three games to one against the Golden State Warriors, forced a game seven. At the end of game seven, the Cavaliers were holding the NBA Championship trophy, ending the 52 year drought and Cleveland's long run of sports frustrations. Very few people outside of the Cleveland locker room believed that this was possible. Down three games to one against the reigning NBA champions and the team that set the all time regular season record for most wins. But the Cavalier players and coaches believed it was possible, and that's all that mattered. Great teams find a connection to a greater purpose, and great teams can answer the question why. A big part of the answer was the loyal fans who stood behind the Cleveland sports teams through heartache and frustration for many years. Lebron and the entire team wanted to bring home a trophy to them. Another thing that struck me as special was the gesture by the Golden State Warrior General Manager Bob Myers. Bob Myers was roaming the arena searching for Cleveland's General Manager David Griffin with the nets from game seven in his hands. In all the chaos, he finally found David Griffin to complete his mission, as tough as that must have been. And what he said showed his class, "They won, and they earned it. So you have to appreciate that. You want to win, but you've got to appreciate what they were able to do and be honored to be a part of it all. I'm just honored to be close to it. It was a great game." And what Bob Myers said next is so powerful, "It's great to go to work and feel this much—good and bad. Most people don't get to feel this much." Let's put what

Bob Myers says in context. He is talking about the game of basketball, and to feel this deeply, good and bad about something. Even though it was the final game of the NBA Championship, it is still a game. Does your profession give you the opportunity to feel this deeply, to make an impact, to serve others, and to truly make a difference? To continue to believe in the power of possibility thinking, even when the odds are stacked against you. There is so much more that can be accomplished when we view the world from the lens of possibility thinking, and I hope all of you strive to find this in your personal as well as professional lives.

In my financial services career possibility thinking motivated me and helped me overcome many of the challenges you face when building a financial services practice. I tried to view all the possibilities whether that was serving clients individually or sharing the career opportunity with a prospective recruit. As time went on and as my career progressed I found great passion in sharing the value a career in financial services can offer. I realized early, to be successful in management and leadership recruiting is paramount, and serves as the building block and foundation for sustainable organizational growth.

MOVING THE RETENTION NEEDLE

Let me share what I found to be invaluable during my leadership career, which consistently produced retention results that were nearly 350% of the industry average. The first thing to understand is that recruiting and selection are not the same. Successful recruiting is all about having an active flow and pipeline of candidates so true selection can take place. In my career, my experience confirmed most managers who have recruiting responsibilities spent more time recruiting and less time selecting. Why? Because their pipeline of viable candidates was thin. So rather than selecting, they had to settle because of a recruiting quota that needed to be met. If you are truly selecting rather than recruiting, you have a much higher probability of predicting the future success of the candidate. This will in turn have a positive effect on retention.

One of the keys to improving retention is to pay close attention to who you are hiring. If the candidate is inexperienced, do they have the talent, skills, and market necessary to be successful? If they're experienced, do they fit your model, your value proposition? Putting a square peg in a round hole rarely if ever works.

When it comes to recruiting and selection, great managers also understand there is an art and a science to it. The "science" comes in the form of psychological and aptitude tests, which definitely serve a purpose. There were two we used during my time in management. The first test was used as our rejection tool, which helped us sort through the entire pool of candidates. The second test was a true selection tool, as it identified the strengths, weaknesses, and individual characteristics of the candidate. This helped us identify whether or not they were a good fit, but also helped determine the areas where extra training and development may be necessary.

As a leader I placed value on both the science and the art of recruiting but many of the judgment calls we made were based on the art side of the equation. Being a skilled interviewer, knowing the right open ended questions to ask can draw out a lot of valuable information. Past success can be a strong indicator of future success. Does the candidate possess a high achievement drive? Hard work alone will not translate to success in the financial services business if certain natural abilities and skill sets are missing. There are many people who have a strong work ethic who shouldn't be in the business.

Another key is to recruit early and to recruit often. In order for this to occur consistently, you have to have a recruiting plan and process. And you have to follow it religiously. Without this, it's easy for recruiting to take a backseat to other demands. The plan should include how many recruits you need each year, and the ratio of names needed to net one hire. This will give you the flow of candidates necessary to reach your annual recruiting goal. Also included in your plan should be your candidate profile and recruiting sources used. Another important part of your plan should detail the number of steps in your recruiting process and who is responsible for each. As the senior leader, I found it very important to involve the entire management team.

Once the initial recruiting interview and aptitude testing was complete, if there was agreement to move to the next step, the candidate was introduced to other members of the team. This also included meeting with key advisors. As we progressed through the selection process, I felt it was important for us to meet their spouse or significant other. I can't recall a time when this step in the process was skipped. Why is this so important? For two simple reasons. First, if you are proud of the organizational culture you've fostered, you want to show it off. You want them to experience it as soon as possible. Secondly, having the candidate and their spouse fully engaged and excited will be essential when they're faced with some of the inevitable emotional ups ands downs a career in financial services presents.

The candidate profile we used included the following:

1. A strong work ethic, a sense of urgency, a drive for achievement, and focus
2. Did they make a good first impression
3. Was I excited to introduce them to our top advisor as a new hire
4. Since this is a sales position, would I buy from them
5. Community involvement
6. A history of success
7. Good communication skills
8. Were they already invested or involved in our business in some way

It's important not to settle. Therefore, you should only want the best of the best on your team. If recruits don't meet your standards, don't hire them. Improving retention begins with good selection. As leaders, we have a responsibility to help those whom we hire become successful. If shortcuts are taken in selection, it will be much more difficult to make good on this promise.

WARM/COLD-SOURCE RECRUITING

I'm a firm believer that the recruiting source matters. Anyone who has direct recruiting responsibilities should have multiple recruiting lines in the water. I also believe most of these lines should be warm. With warm sourcing, you have more control over who you're talking to and the outcome you're looking for is more predictable. The reason it's more predictable is your warm referral network has the candidate profile which describes who you're looking for. It reminds me of a recruiting interview early in my management career. I can't recall the recruiting source used but it wasn't warm. The candidate showed up at the office riding a bicycle. When I asked him about it his response was, I lost my license due to numerous traffic violations. That interview didn't last long.

We tried to be very deliberate about tracking the number of referrals necessary to net one hire. We would consistently run a ratio of eight names to one hire. We also knew the number went up exponentially when cold-source recruiting was added to the mix.

BUILDERS CLUB

During my career, we used three primary recruiting sources, the most important being our "Builders Club". I called this "inside the circle recruiting." Our Business Center was a pioneer in establishing Builders Club, and over the years, this was adopted by many other Business Center's within our company. I called this inside the circle recruiting because the referrals came from advisors and staff within our organization. Each year we tracked the results of our Builder's Club. We knew we could rely on between 50 and 60% of our recruits coming from this source. So if our recruiting goal for the year was 16, we had confidence that 8 to 10 hires would come directly from Builder's Club. And the reason we had confidence is that we had compiled the data over many years, underscoring again the importance of organizational metrics.

Let me share why I feel Builder's Club was so successful for us. Within our recruiting plan, we had a specific Builder's Club strategy each year. The most important question you have to answer for your advisors and staff is Why? Why is this so important to the success of the organization they are all a part of.

This is key because it ties into the culture that you as a leader have built or are trying to build. So if the advisors have not bought into your vision, and if your culture is in need of repair, it will be difficult for your advisors and staff to get on board. Culture transcends everything within the organization. If advisors are willing to refer, this is a strong indication they feel good about the culture you've built.

So this is a start, but it's not enough. To have an engaged Builder's Club, you need to be intentional and you need to make it fun. The responsibility for the execution of our Builder's Club was placed in the hands of one of our key staff members. Each year she would create a theme around Builder's Club and this was announced at our annual kick-off meeting and promoted throughout the year.

One year our theme was "Builder's Club-Building our future one brick at a time." Our staff would show up in hard hats wearing tool belts to showcase our theme. Our goal was to get as many club members as possible. We made this a big deal. To enter the club, you needed to refer at least one individual that went through our testing and selection process. As a member, they were invited to special social events. In addition, they received special recognition as well as marketing dollars and additional staff support to help them grow their business.

Over the years we found Builder's Club to be the single greatest source for referrals. We also found the rewards, recognition, and perks were appreciated but they weren't the primary reason advisors referred. They referred because they bought into our vision. Successful people want to be a part of something successful. This is when we knew we were building something special. All the hard work put in by so many was beginning to pay off. It was validation the culture in our organization was something people wanted to be a part of.

Another important action step in our Builder's Club strategy, we needed to know the best way to obtain names from our advisors and staff and how often we should be asking. We found that, for the most part, once a quarter was the answer. Its important during this meeting no other business or issues were up for discussion. It was important to keep this strictly focused on Builder's Club. We also found that, for this to be successful, the Builder's Club mechanics and calendar had to be run by a key staff member.

We put a lot of time and energy into Builder's Club for the simple reason: if we were able to execute, the quality of new hires was top notch, and the retention of those hired was significantly better.

Another key recruiting source was our COI, or Center of Influence program. I called this "outside the circle" recruiting. COI members were not part of the organization, but they held positions of responsibility in our community: attorneys, cpa's, business owners. Our COI's understood our value proposition, and they believed in the mission and integrity of our organization.

Our yearly recruiting plan included a specific COI strategy that we reviewed each month. The strategy included how each COI meeting would be run, as well as how many COI meetings we would net per month. We found the COIs to be extremely busy people, so having an agenda prepared for each meeting was essential. The meetings were relatively simple affairs-a coffee meeting limited to 30 minutes. The short agenda helped set the tone, kept the pace quick, and respected the time of those we were meeting with.

One thing each COI was always asked was whether or not they wanted to join our COI network. If they wanted us to stay in contact, under what capacity and how often? Our goal was to have four contacts, or "touches" per year, with two of those touches being face-to-face. We hosted a COI appreciation evening in the fall of each year, typically a wine and cheese event, to say thanks and show our appreciation. When we received a referral from a COI, they received a handwritten note of thanks from our leadership team.. And when a COI referral ended up joining us, they'd receive a gift card for dinner on us.

You will not build a successful recruiting program without a specific strategy coupled with team accountability to your goals. The reason we put so much time and attention around these two initiatives, our Builder's Club and COI program, we knew they would deliver the majority of the recruits we needed to reach our yearly goal. This is the result of our quality approach to recruiting. The high turnover of the financial services business necessitates a robust recruitment process. Our in-house organizational culture, as illustrated by Builder's Club and COI program, ensures that ours is not just a recruitment process but a very fine-tuned selection process as well. It's a simple and powerful system with built-in incentives and quality control mechanisms. With the right focus on sourcing, coupled with accountability to the activities necessary to drive the desired recruiting outcome, you can significantly enhance the personnel of your organization and strengthen its culture.

They continue to be the two best recruiting sources within the industry. so why aren't more organizations successfully executing these two strategies. My opinion is: it takes planning. It takes a specific strategy. But most importantly it takes a commitment to the weekly activities necessary to drive the desired outcome. In other words, it takes a lot of hard work. It's easier to buy a list of names or hire an outside company to send you resumes. But the best leaders understand that recruiting is a contact sport, and you need to stay street active all the time. Why would you delegate something this important to someone else? I also recognize the business has changed over the years. I may be a little old fashioned but I do recognize that it's important to have a strong social media presence. This includes Linked-In and Facebook. It's the easiest way to connect to Gen-Xers and Millenials.

The third recruiting source we used was personal observation. My goal was to be the most recognizable face within our organization. Being active in the community, serving on boards, and giving back are things that I've always believed in and found to be very important. This is something I expected the entire leadership team to embrace. There are three positive things that come from being involved: first you give back and make a difference. Second, you strengthen your firm's brand. And third, I can guarantee you'll find opportunities to recruit and share your career story.

To be a successful recruiter, you need to embrace and commit to the following key philosophies:

1. Recruiting is the momentum builder in our business.
2. You must adopt a philosophy of high standards, and never settle
3. Recruit early and often. Commit to having 75% of your recruits hired by July 1st each year, and 100% by October 1st
4. Commit to making Builder's Club your number one recruiting source. This will lead to a systematic flow of referrals from advisors and staff

5. Build your pipeline to a minimum of 25 potential
    candidates, and have a system in place to manage
    the flow

There are many opinions and philosophies when it
comes to recruiting experienced advisors. Our philosophy
was to focus on building our organization through the
recruitment of talented inexperienced individuals. We
believed if we recruited our own advisors, they would be
loyal, coachable, and they would buy into the vision of our
organization.

However, there are forces within the financial services
industry today that have created opportunities to enter into
recruiting discussions with experienced advisors. Over the
years we we're successful in recruiting many key advisors
who ultimately joined our organization. Many times, the
key experienced advisor is easy to spot but difficult to
recruit.

I'll share a quick story that illustrates my point. One of
the most successful experienced advisors who ultimately
joined our organization took me four years to recruit. I was
introduced to Mike by one of our advisors who had a personal as well as professional relationship with him. What
made this challenging is Mike had been with the same
company for nearly 20 years and was extremely loyal. Isn't
that what we all want? Advisors who are loyal and engaged
with us. Over the course of several meetings with Mike, he
began to share more and more with me. Although he was
loyal, there were some threads of discontent and frustrations he started to talk about. What made this even more

challenging was Mike lived more than 600 miles from me. He lived within the territory I was responsible for but not in the same city or even state. I would travel to Mike's city of residence quarterly and prior to each trip would call ahead to see if Mike had 30-45 minutes to see me. Invariably this resulted in me seeing Mike two to three times a year. Over the course of two or three years I developed a friendship with Mike and his family. I got to know his wife Lisa, and they trusted me. Mike would always say, "if I ever leave the company I've been with for 20 years the only place I will go is with you." Mike had his own office and lived several hundred miles from his company's main office. I asked him how many times each year his manager came to see him. His answer was telling. He said his manager had not been to see him in eight years. And my response was, I see you two to three times a year and you're not even part of our organization. I had developed enough trust with Mike by this time I felt I could tell him anything. I said, I'm done having coffee and I'm done buying you lunch. There is no reason in the world why you shouldn't be part of our organization. Are we going to get this done. He made the commitment during that meeting and was part of our team 90 days later. I guess the moral of the story is you never give up on the potential to recruit a number one draft choice. But they can certainly try your patience.

When recruiting experienced advisors we found it helpful to begin by building a profile of the experienced advisor you'd like to recruit. Once you build the profile, share it with the advisors in your organization. Maybe someone on your team already has a personal relationship with who you want to recruit. See if they would be willing to make a personal introduction or, better yet, see if they would be willing to be part of the initial meeting.

It's important to identify what you're looking for when recruiting an experienced advisor. For example, do they fit your value proposition from a business perspective? Do you like and respect them? Do you feel they'll be a good cultural fit. What is their pattern of success and how long have they been in the business? It's also very important to find out why they would consider making a company change. What is their thread of discontent?

There are many reasons today why an experienced advisor may be looking to change companies. I've found that many times, it has to do with significant change that's occurring within their current company. And they're concerned about the company's ability to continue to support their practice or their passion. Whatever the reason, it's crucial to find out why, and do proper due diligence to convince yourself they belong in your organization.

It takes great leadership to build a Master Agency. The three constants which must be present are the attraction of advisors, the development of advisors, and the retention of advisors. You're well on your way to success if you set high standards. are purpose driven, and cast a vision that people believe in and want to be a part of.

10

DEVELOP, DON'T JUST TRAIN

I've shared my thoughts on how you impact retention, its by focusing on selecting, not just recruiting. The second half of the equation is you have to not only train but you have to develop your people. You have to be intentional about this. if you select well, and develop well, you will have a significant impact on increasing retention within your organization.

It begins with having a blueprint and process in place to manage your training and development. Educating and training your advisors should be a top priority. Our view was training is short term, and development is ongoing. We believed in life-long learning, encouraging all our advisors to be students of the business. Our goal was to give each new advisor foundational training during their first 90-120 days in the business. We conducted a fast-start school during the advisors first full week. Our focus during the initial training was not on product knowledge, but on the fundamentals of the business. How to make a phone call with a prospect and secure an appointment on a favorable basis. Working through the objections they might encounter during the phone call, and role-playing how to overcome them. We did a lot of skill building and role-playing during the early phases of training in an effort to build their confidence. The goal during the first week of training was to get brilliant at the basics. How to successfully make a phone call, how to conduct the initial interview with a prospect. How to gain rapport with the prospect and put them at ease, as well as educate them on the planning tool we used. Again, we were very intentional during this first week of training. To view our initial approach from a value-driven perspective, not a product driven process. The first week was devoted to the soft skills necessary to be successful. And we spent a significant amount of time on skill building and role playing.

This sequence of training seemed to work best for us. At times this was challenging because very little if any product training was introduced during the first week. We had to convince new associates to trust us because they really wanted to learn about the products. Our philosophy was pretty simple: if they couldn't set appointments, or if they were afraid to get on the phone, we needed to find this out early. If you can't get in front of people and complete the fact-finding step, all the product training and product knowledge in the world wouldn't matter.

One of their first assignments during the initial week of training was to set a minimum of 10 fact-finding appointments for the second week. These were joint appointments conducted with a member of our management team assisting. So the second week was spent in the field completing as many initial interviews with prospects as possible. But we were very specific about the goal of 10 being the minimum. You want the goal to be specific, you want it to be measurable, and you want it to be time bound. This is critical. We wanted to set the activity expectation early. And we knew if they could consistently set 10 appointments a week they would have the activity necessary to be successful.

The third week we had our recruits back in training to review all the appointments they conducted. Up to this point the entire focus was on phoning, setting appointments, and successfully completing the fact-finding necessary to put a financial plan together. And the interviews were conducted jointly with a member of management. During the third week we introduced the insurance and investment products we marketed using the actual fact-finders that were completed the second week. We found the more we could use real life examples the easier it was for them to see where the specific products apply. During the third week much skill building and role-playing was still used with the focus now being on how to handle the second client appointment. How to present the financial plan, how to overcome objections or concerns the prospect may have. Our goal was to make sure the initial fact-finding interview as well as the demonstration and closing interviews were modeled correctly from the very beginning.

Remember training is short term and development is long term. The entire training program was completed within the first 90-120 days. By the end of this they knew how to successfully make a phone call and secure an appointment on a favorable basis. They knew how to overcome the objections faced when making calls, and how to handle this professionally. They knew how to complete a financial fact-finder, put the case together, and present it to the prospect. They had a fundamental understanding of the financial products we offered, how to represent the company, and how to build a financial services clientele. Also included was training on business conduct and ethics. Weekly assessments were conducted by our Director of Development during the first four months to make sure they were effectively managing all aspects of what was required of them. At the completion of their initial training each recruit had to successfully demonstrate a thorough understanding of all material in order to graduate to the next phase of development.

We had a system in place for training inexperienced recruits and we did not deviate from it. For experienced advisors we customized the training and development to fit what was appropriate for their professional background and experience. This step is extremely important when hiring experienced advisors. The tendency is to think they have already gone through all the training and development they need to be successful. The tendency is to think that once they are contracted all the heavy lifting is over. It's actually just the opposite. Just because they signed a contract to represent your company and sell your products doesn't mean the production will automatically follow. To the experienced advisor, ease of doing business is one of their top priorities. If it's not easy for them to do business with you, they'll take the path of least resistance and continue to do business where it is easy and familiar. Where they have existing relationships.

I feel there were several things that contributed to our organization consistently being recognized as the company leader when it came to new, experienced advisor production.

1. We said what we would do and followed through on every promise made. A strong relationship was formed with the advisor and their staff from the very beginning.
2. Training and education took place immediately on our business systems and process.
3. Introduction to the product platform, both risk and investment based. I wanted our product wholesalers to form strong relationships immediately.
4. A conversation early in the process was held regarding expectations. What they could expect from us, and what we expected from them. This included production, business center involvement, and meeting attendance. This is your chance as a leader to affirm business center standards and expectations. Omitting this step is a big mistake.

Whether your focus is on recruiting inexperienced or experienced advisors, its important to have a blueprint and a roadmap for the training, education, and development of the advisors you are hiring. As leaders, this is part of the promise we make when we extend the opportunity for someone to join our organization.

11

BUILDING A CULTURE OF ACCOUNTABILITY

Having a culture of accountability and high expectations is necessary to have long term success. As a leader you have to make a conscious choice to raise your standards, and this begins with setting standards for what you feel is acceptable behavior for yourself and then modeling this for others. It is absolutely necessary to have a baseline of what you are willing to accept and to clearly communicate this to every individual in your organization. If you don't do this it will be easy for people to slip into attitudes or behaviors that produce results far below what you want and what you deserve. There's a big difference between being interested in something and being committed to it. If you are committed to raising your standards you accept no excuses. This commitment helps you get past the excuses in business or in life that hold you back. Removing the excuses gives you the freedom to accomplish the personal and professional goals you desire for yourself and others.

As the leader it is your responsibility to let your advisors know what is expected of them, and the minimum standards necessary for them to be a part of your organization. I'm a firm believer that measurement improves performance. It tells whether or not you are making progress towards your monthly, quarterly, and yearly goals. When you are keeping score it tells you early in the process if you are off course so corrective measures can be taken to get you back on course. Once you have established and communicated your standards, no exceptions can be made, short of some extenuating circumstance. Its important to understand you can talk all day long about your standards, but the reality is you have set the bar based on what you are willing to accept from your lowest performer. The law of limited performance kicks in quickly, and your advisors soon discover what you are willing to accept as their leader. Having a cadence of accountability is where execution happens; whether at the firm or advisor level. Most years we found the plan fairly easy to come up with. But consistently executing on the plan is difficult. When we failed to execute, invariably we had taken our eye off accounting for the things that mattered most.

PERFORMANCE-POTENTIAL GAP

My fascination with the performance-potential gap really dates back to my collegiate running days. I was always amazed that some runners, who appeared to have less talent, could consistently finish in front of those who were more gifted. Whether athletics or business, why do some individuals through performance get so close to their true potential, while others settle for results far below what they are capable of. Because the differences are small. The tiny so slight differences that give the great an edge. But what exactly are those incremental changes that can impact performance so dramatically? Are they purely physical, or are they achieved through mental and emotional discipline? One of the things I found was top performers were committed to executing consistently regardless of the circumstances. They had the discipline to hold themselves to a higher standard. They used adversity as fuel. It's a lot easier to achieve success when things are comfortable, but what about when things get turned upside down. They were able to use the adversity to take them to a place they wouldn't otherwise go. I found that top performers also embraced coaching and the importance of accountability. They wanted to know at all times whether or not they were winning. They understood that by focusing on the right activities consistently, they could drive the desired outcome. As a leader I also found it energizing to work with individuals who wanted to close the gap between their performance and their potential.

I learned a valuable leadership lesson from my friend Harry Hoopis, GAMA Hall of Fame Inductee and icon in the insurance and financial services industry. Harry would often talk about advisors who have the desire to perform at a high level but something is holding them back. It's your responsibility as their leader to find out what that is. Sometimes its additional training and education that is needed, or role-playing to help sharpen the skills necessary to perform at a higher level. And sometimes it's helping build a stronger belief system and the confidence that's required to perform among the best. Harry would talk often about managing the middle of your organization. Everyone knows you can rely on basically 80 percent of your results coming from the top 20 percent of your people. Its also true the remaining 20 percent will come from 80 percent of your people. When dealing with the middle 60 percent, Harry would say don't lose sight of the 30 percent who want to join the top 20 percent. They are already leaning to the right and have the desire and motivation to get there. Find out what is holding them back and give them the tools and resources to overcome it. If you are successful you will move the performance needle significantly and will now have 50 percent of your organization helping you build a culture where high standards and professional success is the norm.

With inexperienced recruits supervision of activity was mandatory. Setting goals, tracking daily activity, and reporting weekly activity is what we expected. We shared with them why this was critically important to their long term success. Each new advisor attended a weekly planning, evaluation, and progress meeting. During this meeting their weekly activity and results were reviewed and discussed. In addition, new activity commitments were made for the following week. With inexperienced advisors we were managing activity, not results. Its easier to cultivate good practices that lead to balanced activity, but sometimes its difficult to control the results. So if you focus on generating healthy activity, and the results are lacking, you need to diagnosis why, so corrective measures can be taken. This fit really well into our philosophy that measurement improves performance.

In addition to the weekly accountability meeting where

the focus was on reviewing activities necessary to be successful, we also hosted a monthly client builder meeting for all new associates. A portion of this meeting was dedicated to peer accountability and reporting. We found this to be a powerful motivator. Each advisor would report the prior months activity and results, and receive constructive feedback from the group. Skill building on a variety of topics as well as case review, also took place.

Each quarter we hosted a day long Study Group meeting for all associates. The primary focus of our Study Group was practice management. Bringing in tools and resources with the goal of helping our advisors continue to grow a more efficient and effective practice. We wanted each Study Group agenda to highlight what was most important to them. So we asked questions, and we listened. Without fail each quarterly meeting included a presentation by one of our advisors, or a successful advisor from another company. Advisors like to hear what other successful advisors are doing to grow their business. So it was important to include them. We also covered new product introductions, marketing initiatives, as well as any compliance information that needed to be discussed. We would typically close the meeting with a motivational speaker. Our focus was to make our quarterly Study Group meeting so meaningful and value driven that all associates would want to attend. Over the years these meetings became a big part of our culture. In addition to a great lineup of speakers, it was also a time for our advisors and staff to see each other and renew friendships. This is especially important if, like ours, your organization is spread out over a large geographical region. You know you are building something special when 80-90 percent of your organization commits to being involved and attends these meetings.

Our signature event each year was our Summit Retreat. This was a three day retreat that was held in a resort location during the summer months. Our leadership team took great pride in this event. We always wanted this to be a first class experience for the advisors and their families. Invitation to attend Summit was contingent upon the advisor meeting a production benchmark. It became more meaningful because they had to perform and actually qualify in order to attend. Each morning was reserved for business sessions where we would bring in outside speakers as well as ask all those in attendance to present on a variety of topics. Over the years I found some of the best talent was right inside the walls of our own organization, and they enjoyed being asked to participate. The afternoons were devoted to recreational activities with each other and other family members. Each evening our leadership team would host a reception, followed by dinner for all attendees. Summit Retreat was a huge culture builder within our organization. During my time in leadership we hosted 26 Summit's in a variety of locations. You can't always tie a bottom line return to everything you do. We felt our Summit Retreat was priceless when it came to building stronger relationships with our key people. It also gave them a chance to get to know each other on an entirely different level. Friendships were forged between the families who attended. And due to our geographical territory this was the one time each year they all had a chance to spend time together. You talk about a culture builder when you get not only the advisors but their families together. How do you put a price tag on that?

Over the years I enjoyed the most success when I visualized my goals, when I imagined them happening, and when I set goals that truly inspired me. I think its true for all of us when we find goals that inspire us, they become a motivating force in our life, and we get excited about the possibility of achieving them. We don't limit our view of what is possible when setting these wildly important goals. But setting the goal is only the beginning. This has to be followed by the development of the plan and the strategies necessary to execute the plan. Another key to being successful is to make sure you are committed to the achievement of the goal, not just interested in it. Leaders think constantly in terms of I can, I will, and I am, and they have the persistence necessary to stay the course. Those that commit and pay the highest price will realize the greatest rewards. I believe it's also important to understand goals alone can be inspirational, but being able to answer the question why you want them in the first place is the real key. If you can answer the question why, it will unlock the drive and determination necessary to persist and achieve.

Our entire leadership team believed in and embraced the importance of annual planning and goal setting. Each year we facilitated a two-day planning retreat in early January. During this retreat organizational goals for the new year were shared. Having clarity of vision and being able to articulate this vision, so there is excitement and buy-in is the mark of a true leader. During our January retreat each advisor and staff member also completed their plan for the new year, with specific strategies, tactics, and action steps necessary to drive the desired outcome. It was then leadership's responsibility to provide a positive environment to help them reach their yearly goals. This included training, development, and coaching. And it included creating and then reinforcing an environment of high expectations and building a culture where mutual respect and trust was shared by all.

GREAT TEAMS FIND A CONNECTION

One of the most challenging and yet most important things a leader has to do is build a strong leadership team. A team that shares a common purpose and vision. That will sacrifice for the good of the team, regardless of who gets the credit. A team that is consistently thinking about this, "How do we build an even bigger and better culture than what exists today." A team where everyone is spending time on what they do best in order to exponentially raise the organization. In my 36 years in leadership, I found these teams to be rare. There is a big difference between a group of individuals who come together once a month for a management meeting, and call themselves a team, and a real team. A real team is purpose driven and synergistic. A real team has only one agenda, and it's not hidden. It's to advance the mission of the entire organization, regardless of who gets the credit. A real team communicates openly and honestly. And a real team respects the rights of each team member. This doesn't mean that team members always agree. Healthy conflict and debate is a good thing, where challenging ideas are shared and discussed; where each team member is encouraged to be creative in their thinking.

If you are in a leadership position, think about what I have shared. Regardless of where you are in your leadership journey be mindful of what it takes to build a successful team, and don't settle. In my leadership career one of the things I felt was very important was to make sure the entire team knew what their strengths were, as well as some areas where they needed to improve. By uncovering the strengths and talents of each team member everyone can focus their time and energy on what they do best. When a team has synergy, when everyone knows their respective role, and takes ownership, it gives you a winning edge. One of the ways to sort out the strengths and talents of your team is through a talent assessment. There are many to choose from, but I found the Gallup "Strength Finder" to be a great assessment tool and resource. Remember, it's important to build a team you believe in, and a team who believes in you as their leader. With the talent that's available there is no reason to ever put yourself in a position to settle for less than what you as well as the organization you lead deserve.

WHAT MATTERS MOST

One of the things over the course of my career that mattered most to me was making sure I created value and made a difference in the lives of those I served. From my

perspective, I would like to share with you what great leaders think about, and what great leaders do.

Great leaders are mindful of what matters most to
those they are leading. Not only from a professional perspective, but personal as well. Great leaders align the best
interests of the organization with the best interests of their
people. When you create a culture that puts your advisors
and the clients they serve first, it will drive a great outcome.
Great leaders focus on people not things. Without talented
people and a great culture, your best-laid plans will fail. As
a leader, establishing a relationship based on mutual
respect and trust is critical. Building a culture that everyone
is proud of and wants to be a part of will not happen if people find it difficult to trust you. Great leaders are transpar-
ent and accountable. When mistakes are made, leaders
don't blink, but take responsibility for their actions. This
helps build trust and rapport with the team they are leading. Great leaders give credit to the team, which instills
confidence and elevates their level of play. Great leaders
are emphatic and seek to understand. It's one of the ways
they show they care. Great leaders inspire a mindset of
winning. They have a track record of producing results.
They know how the game is played, and they play to the
strengths of their team in order to win. As a result, the
teams they lead are consistently recognized as the best.
Great leaders get outside their paradigm and they inspire
others to do the same. When they look at hardship, they
see opportunity. And rather than fear change, they
embrace it. Great leaders look for a connection to a greater
purpose, which the entire team can share. Their passion,

their mission, and their desire to make a difference and leave a legacy are what make them truly special.

12

The End is the Beginning

I've tried to live my life as a journey. Taking in and learning from all the experiences and opportunities God has provided. As I traveled this journey I found myself becoming more introspective and conscious in my thinking. Maybe this is a natural progression. Questions such as, "What's the purpose of my life and my leadership?" "Will I leave a legacy behind? Will it matter? To whom?" I've tried to live my life with passion and purpose, following leadership principles that would make my parents proud. I owe so much to them for the sacrifices they made, and for the positive influence they played in my life. I think more about these questions today than I ever did before. And maybe I'm coming to some conclusions about a few things.

John Wooden, the great UCLA basketball coach, said, "You can't live a perfect day without doing something for someone who will never be able to repay you." How much better would the world be if we all made a commitment to do this. But what happens is thinking like this, I'm only one person and what can one person do to truly make a difference. And the answer is you can do more than you ever thought possible. It's the actions of ordinary people doing extraordinary things and the desire to leave a legacy that can move mountains. It's having the courage to take a stand for what you believe in and for understanding our legacy lives on in people, not things. But too often we put our time, our energy, and our attention into systems or buildings or other projects—but only people live on after we are gone. Everything else is temporary. So make sure the people closest to you, your inner circle, know how much you love and appreciate the sacrifices they have made. After all, most of us wouldn't be where we are if someone wasn't paying the price to help us reach our true potential.

My professional career spanned 35 years, all with the Principal Financial Group. What a blessing it was to be a part of a company with strong values and high ethical standards. There were professional accomplishments in my career that truly stand out in my mind. But it's easy to speak about what stands above them all: the opportunity I had to work with my brother for 34 years stands alone. He was a great partner who shared my passion and vision for building an organization that was special. Thanks brother for walking side by side with me, and for understanding why it's the people we lead that matter most.

How do you put into words what transpires in the span of 35 years? It's a beautiful book filled with many highs and a few lows. The advisors and families who were a part of our organization, who helped expand and deepen our mission of making a difference each day, made our organization such a special place to be. The hall of fame inductions. The new births and birthdays. High school and college graduations. Weddings and anniversaries are all things that I will remember and cherish forever. And those who have passed on will never be forgotten.

And to my family. To my wife Patty, who has shared this journey with me. Thanks for being such a wonderful mother and grandmother to our children and grandchildren. And for being there with me through the ups and downs, always maintaining a positive outlook, and modeling for me what purpose-driven servant leadership is all about.

To my three children: Kristin, Laura, and Garrett. You always worked hard to make your dad proud. You never disappointed me. And now you are young adults, making a difference in the world each day—what more could a father ask.

And to all of you who are striving to find meaning and purpose in your life, let me leave you with this. Steven Covey, a man of great purpose and wisdom, teaches that we will all travel one of two roads in life. The young and the old, the rich and the poor, men and women alike. One is the broad well-traveled road of mediocrity. The other is the road to greatness and meaning. And the range of possibilities that exist within each of these two destinations is as wide as the diversity of gifts and personalities in the human family. But the contrast, the contrast between the two destinations is as the night is to the day.

So my hope for all of you is that you will choose—because it is a choice. That you will choose the road to greatness and meaning. That you'll find the purpose in your life. That you'll make a difference in the lives of those who you serve.

PRAISE FOR
BREAKING THE TAPE

"I have known Cliff for many decades both personally and in the business world. Words that come to mind in describing Cliff have to do with his passion and life's purpose. He is Principled, Focused, Family First, Humble, Physical Fitness, Ethical, Value Driven, Intellect with Business Savvy, Forward Thinker, and Faith Filled. He has touched my life and the lives of others in so many positive ways. He is one great person with much to share. He is a person that if in a fight I would want in my Foxhole."

Frank I. Kintzle, CLU, CHFC, CFP, CEBS, MSM
Principal Financial Group Hall of Fame

"It is always enlightening to read insights on leadership that were forged in the heat of the real world, business setting. That's what we have in Cliff Karthauser. On top of that, his personal values make him the kind of leader anyone would love to have their son or daughter work for and learn from. Cliff's combination of drive, integrity, and genuine commitment to the success of others makes him a rare commodity."

Kim Hoogeveen, Ph.D.
President & CEO
MindSet LLC

"Cliff Karthauser is a first class proven leader and professional in business and in life. Cliff is a tremendous developer of people in helping them achieve extraordinary results by leading by example and modeling the way. His tremendous success in business and in life are due to his tireless work ethic, excellent leadership skills, high achievement drive, strong business acumen and his caring about people and outcomes."

Nick Cecere
Sr. Vice President
Principal Financial Group

"Cliff Karthauser is one of the most focused, passionate and purposeful leaders I have ever met! His strong values, work ethic, commitment to family and faith shine through in Breaking the Tape. Cliff has stood on the shoulders of those great leaders who came before him and created an incredible legacy of inspiration, influence and impact for generations of new leaders. It's been an honor to watch Cliff inspire others' lives and careers for over 20 years! God bless!"

Terri O'Halloran
Vice President, Client Development
Integrity Solutions

"An organization's purpose should be defined by its leader and expanded into every facet of that business. Associated with Cliff for over 30 years, I have personally witnessed that his transformational style is a declaration of purpose driven leadership. "Breaking the Tape" will allow its readers to clarify their purpose and make it the essence of who they are and how they lead."

L E Reelitz, CLF, RICP
Regional Managing Director
Principal Financial Group
GAMA Hall of Fame Inductee

"Cliff is an inspirational leader and has been an important role model for me professionally and personally. He understands the true meaning of leadership and the impact purpose driven leadership can have on building a healthy work culture and a successful business. Breaking the Tape is an opportunity for you to learn how to be a more effective leader.

Patricia Kearns
President & CEO
Quality Living, Inc.

"I never think about setting a national record in the 880 yard run in 1971. What I do often think about is standing on the track at Burke Stadium in Omaha, Nebraska, before it happened. While Cliff grabbed my sweats, the coach of the runner next to me said, 'He's never been beaten.' My brother quickly replied, 'Not until today.' That determined the outcome before the race was even run. I would win that day and I would run faster than anyone my age had ever run before. In that moment, the hard part was done; the easy part was the running. Cliff's three simple words illustrate that leaders don't need big speeches to impact outcomes."

Gary L. Karthauser
Regional Managing Director
Principal Financial Group

"Cliff is the most impactful leader I have ever worked with. His passion for people and drive for success are second to none. Simply put, I'm a better person and professional thanks to his leadership and influence."

Richard C. Jackson, CFP
President
First Heartland Capital, Inc.

"Cliff knows a lot about leadership and now he is telling all in "Breaking the Tape". It's never your own strength that helps you succeed, but instead it's the Strength of the Purpose that leads us. This is a must read for all those who hope to succeed in their chosen career!"

Harry P. Hoopis | Chief Executive Officer
Hoopis Performance Network
GAMA Hall of Fame Inductee

"I've known Cliff for more than thirty years. His leadership capabilities are extraordinary. Cliff has achieved in every area of his life and has done so by having a sense of purpose. His transferable skills presented in this book will provide you with a roadmap to being the best you can be. A must-read for all leaders!"

Richard Kimmel
Regional Managing Director
Principal Financial Group

"Cliff has consistently demonstrated the highest level of leadership for many years. Through the gift of his book you can learn from the master and be inspired by the passion that drove Cliff to be successful and world class as an athlete, in his professional career and most importantly in life. Cliff's book provides a powerful message relating to the ups and downs of life and how a leader can take personal responsibility to achieve to their highest level. This book is a must read!"

Boyd Ober
President & CEO, Leadership Resources
Author–Magnitude: Releasing the Power of
Your Leadership Presence

"Cliff is a unique kind of leader. Cliff is one of those leaders who will do anything it takes to model leadership versus talking about it. A servant leader strives to outwork those who follow and Cliff is certainly a perfect example of that. While his success spans across many industries, his focus remains the same. Cliff strives to serve. Through doing so he has accomplished more than most will in a life time and he's just getting started."

Dan Allison
President
Brokers Clearing House, Ltd.
Author—Feedback Marketing

"Cliff Karthauser has been part of the Fellowship of Christian Athletes leadership for more than 20 years as a part of our board at the state and area levels. Cliff is committed to be a servant-leader in his relationships with people, which is the indispensable quality of great leadership. That combined with his many years of experience in leadership roles has been a great blessing not only to the FCA as an organization but also to me personally. I think you will be blessed by the reading of this book."

Chris Bubak
Nebraska State Director
Fellowship of Christian Athletes

"Breaking the Tape is excellent work! The reading is rhythmic, captures the reader to the point of wanting more. Cliff Karthauser writes in the same manner he lives his life, with passion. I've known Cliff for over 30 years and his reputation is one of excellence and outstanding leadership yet retains a high degree of humility and thankfulness for his opportunities in life. This book is a great read with many lessons and at the end you'll understand how passion plays a great role in leadership. I'm blessed to have a friend like Cliff."

George J Follstad, CLU
Regional Managing Director
Principal Financial Group

"If improving your leadership skills is your desire, then Cliff Karthauser is someone you should listen to. Cliff has successfully and modestly attained success through sports as a competitive distance runner and through business as an Executive with Principal Financial Group. Cliff is a renowned motivational speaker and of course, a family man extraordinaire. His friendship, guidance and encouragement have helped me improve the leadership culture within our company. I am greatly appreciative."

Michael McGillick
President–Essex Corporation